# REPTILE

Madagascan
chameleon

Soft-shelled turtle

Jackson's chameleon

Indian
python

Starred tortoise

DK EYEWITNESS BOOKS

Radiated tortoise

# REPTILE

Written by
COLIN McCARTHY

Sinaloan milk snake

Basilisk lizard

Red-eared terrapin

Caiman

Eyed lizard

DK

Dorling Kindersley

Tree skink

Tegu lizard

# Dorling Kindersley

**LONDON, NEW YORK, AUCKLAND, DELHI, JOHANNESBURG, MUNICH, PARIS and SYDNEY**

## For a full catalog, visit

DK www.dk.com

Project editors  Gillian Denton and Lynne Williams
**Art editor**  Neville Graham
**Senior editor**  Helen Parker
**Senior art editors**  Jacquie Gulliver and Julia Harris
**Production**  Louise Barratt
**Picture research**  Kathy Lockley
**Special photography**  Karl Shone, Jane Burton,
Kim Taylor, and Colin Keates

This Eyewitness ® Book has been conceived by
Dorling Kindersley Limited and Editions Gallimard

© 1991 Dorling Kindersley Limited
This edition © 2000 Dorling Kindersley Limited
First American edition, 1991

Published in the United States by
Dorling Kindersley Publishing, Inc.
375 Hudson Street,
New York, NY 10014
4 6 8 10 9 7 5

Dorling Kindersley books are available at special discounts for
bulk purchases for sales promotions or premiums. Special
editions, including personalized covers, excerpts of existing
guides, and corporate imprints can be created in large
quantities for specific needs. For more information, contact
Special Markets Dept., Dorling Kindersley Publishing, Inc.

**Library of Congress Cataloging-in-Publication Data**
McCarthy, Colin.
Reptile / written by Colin McCarthy;
photographs by Karl Shone, Jane Burton,
Kim Taylor, and Colin Keates.
p. cm — (Eyewitness Books)  Includes index.
Summary: Photographs and text depict the many different
kinds of reptiles, their similarities and
differences, habitats, and behavior.
1. Reptiles — Juvenile literature. [1. Reptiles.]
I. Keates, Colin, ill. II. Shone, Karl, ill. III. Title.
QL644.2.M32  2000  597.9 — dc20  90-4890
ISBN 0-7894-5787-3 (pb)         ISBN 0-7894-5786-5 (hc)

Color reproduction by Colourscan, Singapore
Printed in China by Toppan Printing Co. (Shenzhen) Ltd.

Caiman

Grass snake

Flying snake

Alligator snapping tu

Corn snake

# Contents

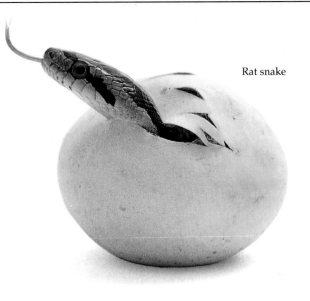

Rat snake

# What is a reptile?

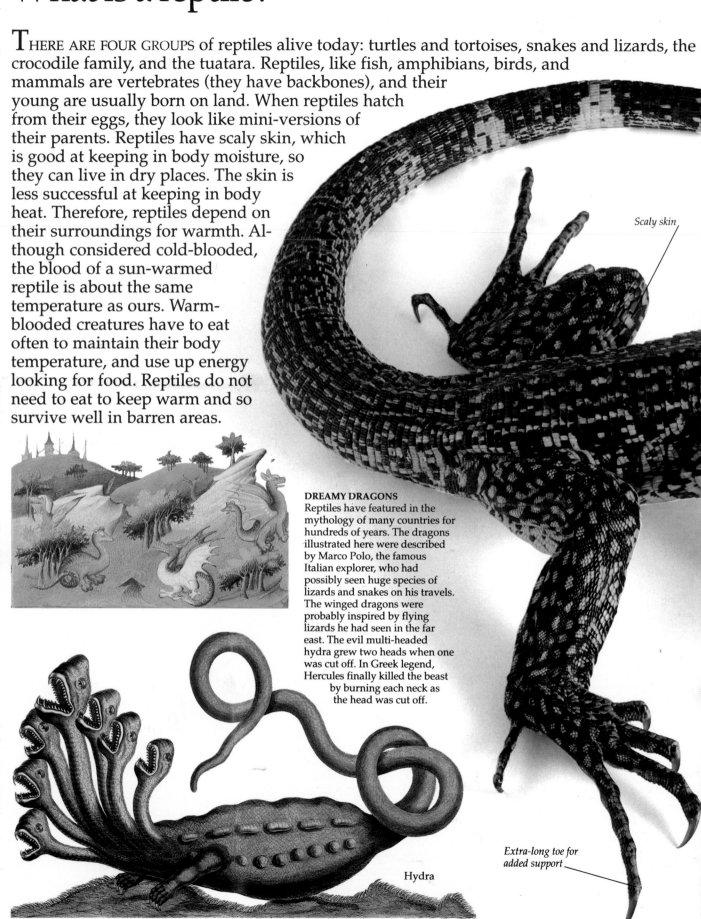

THERE ARE FOUR GROUPS of reptiles alive today: turtles and tortoises, snakes and lizards, the crocodile family, and the tuatara. Reptiles, like fish, amphibians, birds, and mammals are vertebrates (they have backbones), and their young are usually born on land. When reptiles hatch from their eggs, they look like mini-versions of their parents. Reptiles have scaly skin, which is good at keeping in body moisture, so they can live in dry places. The skin is less successful at keeping in body heat. Therefore, reptiles depend on their surroundings for warmth. Although considered cold-blooded, the blood of a sun-warmed reptile is about the same temperature as ours. Warm-blooded creatures have to eat often to maintain their body temperature, and use up energy looking for food. Reptiles do not need to eat to keep warm and so survive well in barren areas.

*Scaly skin*

**DREAMY DRAGONS**
Reptiles have featured in the mythology of many countries for hundreds of years. The dragons illustrated here were described by Marco Polo, the famous Italian explorer, who had possibly seen huge species of lizards and snakes on his travels. The winged dragons were probably inspired by flying lizards he had seen in the far east. The evil multi-headed hydra grew two heads when one was cut off. In Greek legend, Hercules finally killed the beast by burning each neck as the head was cut off.

Hydra

*Extra-long toe for added support*

# What is not a reptile?

At first glance, the salamander looks like a lizard, however, it is not a reptile but an amphibian. Amphibians, for example frogs and toads, are often mistaken for reptiles, though they belong to a different class of animals. Amphibians are unlike reptiles in many ways. They have no scales and breathe through their skin. The skin is kept moist by special mucus glands. Most frogs, toads, and salamanders need to be near water when they breed. They often lay their eggs in water, where the tadpoles then hatch. This European fire salamander, however, keeps her eggs inside her body until seconds before hatching, when she gives birth to live tadpoles directly into the water.

Fire salamander

Like all frogs, this monkey frog is an amphibian. Unlike reptiles, most frogs have smooth, moist skin and no scales.

*External ear*

*Tail helps balance*

*Eye with movable eyelid*

*Many reptiles have special tongues*

### TEGU LIZARD
Reptiles come in all sorts of shapes and sizes. Lizards are one of the biggest and most varied groups. Tegu lizards come from tropical South America. This is a young tegu, but as tegus age, they get fatter from their diet of young birds, mammals, and even other lizards. The tegu's skin is covered with horny, dead scales which are good at keeping in the body's fluids. The tegu's eyelids are movable like most other lizards. However, some geckos, and most snakes, cannot blink, as their eyes are protected by a solid, transparent window. The feet of many reptiles give a good clue to the animals' life-style. They may be used for clambering over smooth surfaces, climbing among swaying stems, or negotiating hot, soft sand dunes. Some burrowing lizards, and most snakes, have no legs.

### LIVING ON LAND
Most reptiles lay eggs (pp. 20–21), though some give birth to live young. Unlike most amphibians, reptiles lay their eggs on land including the reptiles which normally spend a great deal of their life in water, such as turtles and crocodiles. Reptiles lay their eggs in a great variety of sites – in sand, in grass, on riverbanks, and in termite mounds. The incubation period is different for each species and is affected by climate.

African grass snake with eggs

# When reptiles ruled the world

## PTEROSAURS
Flying reptiles, or pterosaurs, dominated the air for over 100 million years, until they became extinct at the same time as the dinosaurs. Their wings were membranes stretched between a single long finger and their legs.

T HE FIRST REPTILES APPEARED some 340 million years ago during the time known as the Carboniferous period. They evolved from amphibians, and although not much is known of their very early history, it seems likely that these first reptiles looked like some of our lizards today. It was not until the later Mesozoic era, 230 to 70 million years ago, that flying reptiles appeared. During this period other reptiles gave up living on land and returned to dominate the seas and lakes, and dinosaurs ruled the land. The reptiles owe their success mainly to their special eggs (pp. 6–7), which, unlike those of amphibians, usually have shells, and do not need to be laid in water. Reptiles themselves were therefore more adaptable and able to live in habitats which would be unsuitable for water-dependent amphibians.

Vertebra of *Palaeophis*, an ancient sea snake

## ANCIENT GIANTS
The enormous vertebrae of an extinct form of sea snake, known as *Palaeophis*, found in West Africa, proved the existence in the Cenozoic era of a snake three to four times the size of a modern python. The vertebra shown here is from a present-day python over 20 ft (6 m) long. Though stories of 65 ft (20 m) long ancient snakes have been reported, such creatures are probably mythical.

Vertebra of a modern python

### TIME CHART OF THE EARTH (Millions of years ago)

| Paleozoic era | | Mesozoic era | | | Cenozoic era |
|---|---|---|---|---|---|
| Carboniferous period | Permian period | Triassic period | Jurassic period | Cretaceous period | Palaeocene period to the present day |
| 350 | 270 | 225 | 190 | 141 | 70 |
| | | Turtles, tortoises, and terrapins | | | |
| | | Crocodilians | | | |
| | | Lizards | | | |
| | | | Snakes | | |

Duration of each period not to scale

## SLOW TO CHANGE
Lizards first appeared about 200 million years ago, evolving alongside dinosaurs. Although rarely found as fossils, there is evidence that different lizards existed before the end of the Mesozoic era. This example, which is 190 million years old, shows the small head, short neck, long body and tail, and sprawling legs that are still typical of the group today.

*Pointed teeth for eating fish*

## OLD CROCS
The crocodile is probably the closest living relative of dinosaurs and seems to have evolved at the same time, during the Triassic period, about 200 million years ago. The sharp, pointed teeth of early crocodiles suggest that they were mostly specialized fish-eaters, unlike most modern species, which sometimes eat plants along with their meat. The basic crocodile skull has changed little.

Ancient crocodile skull

## DOG-JAW
This skull with its doglike jaws belonged to a meat-eating reptile called *Cynognathus*. This four-footed creature was an advanced form of the mammal-like reptiles, which dominated land animals through much of the Permian and Triassic periods. It was from this group of reptiles that mammals evolved about 195 million years ago.

*Skull of* Cynognathus

*Strong jaw and large teeth for meat-eating*

...construction of an advanced ...mmal-reptile showing an improved ...sprawling posture

## ...RTLE FIRST
...fossilized remains of the first recognizable turtle were ...nd in rocks some 200 million years old. Although never one ...he dominating reptiles, the turtle's structure was flexible ...ugh to cope with the many changes in the environment that ...e taken place since it evolved. This adaptability has allowed ...les to develop successful land and aquatic forms, and to ...ome the oldest living group of reptiles.

## TOOTHLESS
The skull of a modern turtle has no roof openings, and there are no teeth in the jaws (pp. 32–33). The skull of *Proganochelys*, which dates from the early Triassic period, shows that the top of the skull has not changed. There are, however, toothlike projections in the roof of the mouth, although they are not visible here.

*Toothless jaws*

# Happy families

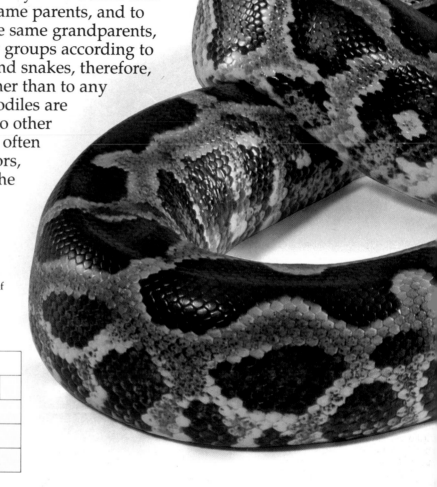

EVOLUTION IS THE BASIS for the classification of animals. In the same way that you are related to your brothers and sisters because you share the same parents, and to your cousins because you share the same grandparents, animals are divided up into family groups according to their common ancestors. Lizards and snakes, therefore, are more closely related to each other than to any other group, but surprisingly, crocodiles are more closely related to birds than to other reptiles. However, because there is often not enough evidence about ancestors, family groupings also depend on the common features of the animals alive today (pp. 6–7).

## REPTILES TODAY

Only four groups of reptiles have managed to survive until modern times. The largest by far are the lizards and the snakes. The others were not always so scarce; fossils of at least 108 species of crocodilians have been found, and the group to which the tuatara belongs was at one time also made up of many more species.

| | | |
|---|---|---|
| | Lizards 3,000 species | |
| | Snakes 2,700 species | |
| | Turtles 200 species | |
| | Crocodilians 23 species | |
| | Tuatara 2 species | |

Monitor lizard

## LIZARDS

Lizards come in many different shapes and sizes. Iguanas, agamas, and chameleons are closely related to each other, and together with geckos form the most primitive lizard group. Girdle-tail lizards, skinks, wall and sand lizards, and whiptails and racerunners are another closely related group. Monitors, beaded lizards, and glass lizards are also grouped together (pp. 28–29).

British Virgin Island gecko

## DAVID AND GOLIATH

The largest reptile in the world is the estuarine or saltwater crocodile. It is an aggressive crocodile and commonly grows to a length of 16 ft (5 m) but specimens as long as 26 ft (8 m) have been recorded. It is found from southern India to northern Australia. The smallest reptile in the world is the British Virgin Island gecko, which is often no longer than 0. 7 in (18 mm).

Estuarine crocodile

## SNAKES

Snakes are legless reptiles with long, slender bodies. There are three groups of snakes: primitive snakes, which include pythons and boas; blind snakes, which include thread snakes; and advanced snakes, which include rear-fanged snakes, cobras, sea snakes, and vipers. Snakes are found all over the world except in very cold areas (pp. 26–27).

Indian python

## TURTLES

Turtles are reptiles with short, broad bodies enclosed in a bony shell. The bone of the shell is usually covered by horny plates, or less commonly, by leathery skin. Turtles are divided into two main groups: hidden-neck turtles, which retract the head and neck into the shell in a vertical S-shaped curve (these include snapping turtles, terrapins, tortoises, sea turtles, and softshell turtles); and side-necked turtles, which bend the neck to the side and hide it under the lip of the shell (these include the snake-necked turtle, the matamata, and African mud turtles).

Hermann's tortoise

## CROCODILIANS

Crocodilians are divided into three families: crocodiles, gavials, and alligators, which includes caimans. They are a very old group of reptiles but in several ways are more advanced than the other groups. They have a much more efficient circulatory system, and according to some, are more intelligent. They also are more attentive to their young (pp. 34–35).

Caiman

# Inside out

In many reptiles, bone growth does not stop at maturity, which means that some reptiles keep growing throughout their lives. If a reptile survives the everyday dangers of life, it may eventually become giant-sized. This is particularly true of pythons, crocodiles, and giant tortoises, though smaller lizards and turtles usually stop growing after they reach a certain size. Also, most reptiles do not lose their teeth when they are old, as mammals do; they shed the old teeth and grow new ones (pp. 38–39).

*Tail vertebra*

*Trunk vertebra*

Unlike a snake, the insides of a lizard are symmetrical (even)

Chameleon skeleton

*Skull*

**CHAMELEON**
Many lizards have highly specialized skeletons. The chameleon, for example, is adapted for life in trees and bushes. The body is broad, providing greater stability when the animal's weight is centered over a narrow twig or branch (pp. 28–29). The fingers and toes are designed for grasping. Each hind leg has three toes on the outside and two on the inside, and each foreleg has just the opposite. The tail is prehensile, that is, tailor-made for grasping.

**CAIMAN**
The caiman's skull is long, and the eye sockets nostrils are set high. In this way, the caiman can float with just its nose and eyes above the water body is long too. It has two pairs of short legs, the toes – five on the front feet and four on the – are partly webbed. The upper jaw of the caima as is true of all other members of the crocodile family, is almost solid bone.

Caiman skeleton

*Skull*

*Ribs*

*Neck vertebra*

*Tail vertebra*

*Ribs*

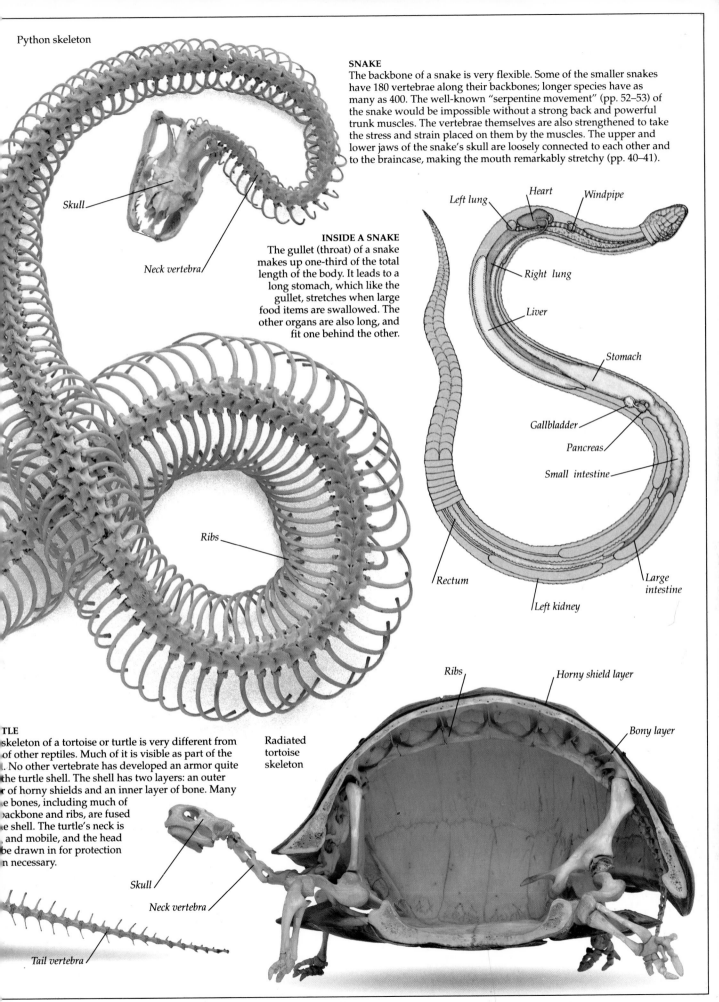

Python skeleton

Skull

Neck vertebra

**SNAKE**
The backbone of a snake is very flexible. Some of the smaller snakes have 180 vertebrae along their backbones; longer species have as many as 400. The well-known "serpentine movement" (pp. 52–53) of the snake would be impossible without a strong back and powerful trunk muscles. The vertebrae themselves are also strengthened to take the stress and strain placed on them by the muscles. The upper and lower jaws of the snake's skull are loosely connected to each other and to the braincase, making the mouth remarkably stretchy (pp. 40–41).

**INSIDE A SNAKE**
The gullet (throat) of a snake makes up one-third of the total length of the body. It leads to a long stomach, which like the gullet, stretches when large food items are swallowed. The other organs are also long, and fit one behind the other.

Left lung

Heart

Windpipe

Right lung

Liver

Stomach

Gallbladder

Pancreas

Small intestine

Rectum

Left kidney

Large intestine

Ribs

Ribs

Horny shield layer

Bony layer

TLE
skeleton of a tortoise or turtle is very different from of other reptiles. Much of it is visible as part of the l. No other vertebrate has developed an armor quite the turtle shell. The shell has two layers: an outer r of horny shields and an inner layer of bone. Many e bones, including much of ackbone and ribs, are fused e shell. The turtle's neck is , and mobile, and the head be drawn in for protection n necessary.

Radiated tortoise skeleton

Skull

Neck vertebra

Tail vertebra

# Cool customers

Reptiles are cold-blooded (pp. 6–7). This means that their temperature changes with that of their surroundings. It takes time for them to adjust to rapid temperature changes, so they live best where the climate is usually hot. To speed the process of warming, a reptile will often bask in the sun. As it warms up, it starts moving in search of food, or even a mate. As the day becomes hotter, the reptile retreats into the shade to cool down. By shuttling backward and forward, in and out of the shade, the reptile can keep a surprisingly constant internal temperature. A reptile needs to stay warm while it is digesting food – a snake that has eaten, but cannot get to a warm place, may die because the food in its stomach will be too cold to digest. In poor weather, reptiles have low body temperatures; they move slowly and are in danger from predators.

Lizard basking in the heat

### KEEPING COOL
In the early morning this agama lizard sits on top of the rock in bright sunlight. After it warms up, it will around looking for insect eat. During the hotte part of the day the agama retreats into shade. If it cools dow too much it will cree back onto the rock in the sun. The pattern warming and coolin down varies with th seasons. For example, during cool months reptiles are only active at midday, when it is w but during the summer month they may go underground at midday to avoid overheating.

Sand lizard

### HOT FOOT
When the ground is too hot for its feet, the sand lizard of the Namib Desert "dances," lifting its legs up alternately from the scorching sand. Sometimes, it rests on its belly, lifting all four legs up at the same time. The little ground gecko is also uncomfortable on the hot sand, but it is mainly nocturnal and is usually out when it is cooler.

Ground gecko

### TAKING IT EASY
Crocodiles cool down by letting moisture evaporate thr their opened mouths, or by simply lying in the cool wat a muddy stream. American crocodiles lie in burrows or when they find the heat too much. On cold nights, croco use the water to stay warm, by sleeping at the bottom o rivers and ponds.

### BOILING OVER
Some people turn r with anger as bloo rushes to their face, their blood temper. does not really rise Committing a deed cold blood" – refer to a callous action – a misinterpretation the term (pp. 6–7).

**ING COVER**

many other desert snakes, the sand viper will do its best to avoid the full
of the day. It is mainly nocturnal and moves in a "sidewinding" fashion
hunts for prey (pp. 52–53). It may travel as much as half a mile (1 km) in a
e night, searching for its favorite food – small mammals and lizards. If it
s to escape the hot midday sun of the deserts of North Africa and Arabia,
mply sinks itself into the sand.

**2 GOING...**
The snake descends vertically,
shuffling and rocking its body. As it goes
down, it shovels sand upward and
over its back. The scales
along the snake help
to work the grains of
sand along its body.

**GOING...**
A sand viper retreats into the sand, tail first,
riggling as it goes. Its eyes are well protected
om irritating grains of sand by the "window"
at covers and shields them.

**3 GONE!**
The sand viper is now almost
ompletely buried. Soon only the
op of its head will be visible.
edding down in the hot desert
and in this way protects it from
he scorching sun, and at the
ame time, makes a perfect
iding place when either
nemies or prey are nearby.

*nake leaves very
isible marks as it
oves in the sand*

# Uncommon senses

REPTILES HAVE SENSES common to vertebrates – smell, sight, and hearing. They also have other ways of finding out about their surroundings. For example, snakes, and some lizards, "smell" with the help of the tongue and the Jacobson's organ – sensory cells in the roof of the mouth. Some snakes are very sensitive to heat given off by living bodies – which means they can detect warm-blooded prey, even in total darkness. Marine turtles navigate immense distances to their nesting beaches, possibly by using the position of the sun. Or, they may be able to follow magnetic fields caused by electric currents in the water. In some reptiles, certain senses are not very highly developed. For instance, most burrowing reptiles have poor eyesight, and snakes do not hear very well.

**ALLIGATOR ROAR**
Alligators communica[te] with one another over vast distances by bellowing. The sound can be very loud, up t[o] 92 decibels at 16 ft (5 [m]) roughly as loud as the propeller engine of a small airplane!

*Swiveling eye is set on a turret*

*Eyelids can close to tiny peepholes*

*Pincer-like toes grasp branches*

**SMALL BUT NOISY**
Most geckos make sounds. Certain species produce chirping and clicking noises, usually when mating or defending territory. When distressed, some lizards even produce ultrasounds, which they use to scare off predators. These sounds are detectable by mammals or birds, but are out of the hearing range of the lizards themselves.

**BROAD HORIZONS**
The chameleon can move its eyes independently and has an extraordinarily wide field of vision. If it sees a fly, it can keep one eye on the fly, while moving toward it. As the chameleon moves, its other eye scans the surroundings, keeping a lookout for possible enemies. When the fly is in range, the chameleon swivels both eyes toward it; at this point the chameleon's eyesight becomes more like the binocular vision of humans. With both eyes firmly fixed on the fly, the chameleon can judge its position more accurately – and take aim.

## SENSITIVE SOULS

Like all animals, snakes have gradually changed, or evolved, over millions of years. At some point they seem to have gone through a burrowing stage, which affected their senses. Their eyesight and hearing became weaker; their other senses became more acute. Snakes have no external ears. Vibrations from the ground simply move along to the inner ear through skull bones that are joined to the lower jaw. Some snakes have special heat detectors. This Indian python has little heat sensitive pits, or holes, in its lips. These are particularly useful for detecting warm-blooded prey, such as mammals or birds, at night (pp. 42–43).

## SIC TO ITS EARS

thousands of years, snakes have been pictured dancing e music of a pipe played by a charmer. This has led to mistaken belief that the snakes are somehow notized by the music. In fact, the snake is rising nsively and following the movement of the e as it prepares to attack it.

*Deeply forked tongue*

*Eye has "glassy" stare because there is no movable eyelid*

## TESTING THE AIR

All lizards have a well-developed, extendable tongue; the tongues of snakes and monitor lizards are deeply forked. They flick in and out, constantly "tasting" chemical particles in the air or on the ground. These particles are transferred from the tip of the tongue to the series of cells in the roof of the mouth called the Jacobson's organ. This organ partly "smells" and partly "tastes" these particles. The specialized tongue can help to trail prey, sample food, find a mate, and detect enemies.

*Nostril*

*Jacobson's organ*

*Tongue*

*Tear duct*

*Eye is protected by transparent solid window*

## SIGHT AND SOUND

anas have very good eyesight. They
can see in color, which explains why
many members of the iguana family
mmunicate by using their colorful head
rnaments, crests, and throat fans. Color is
lso important for many lizards as a way of
tinguishing between the sexes. Iguanas, and
st lizards, can hear airborne sounds through
ble ear openings. The ear drum is very near the
surface of the surrounding skin; in mammals it is
und in a deep "earhole." Although a typical lizard
ear better than a snake, which only hears vibrations
from the ground, it cannot hear as well as a human.

# Dating displays

REPTILES SPEND MOST OF THEIR TIME in day-to-day survival, adjusting body heat, searching for food, and escaping from predators. During the mating season, however, they need to be able to attract members of the opposite sex, in order to reproduce. Male lizards often display bright colors and ornate features such as frills and crests to appeal to the females. As in the rest of the animal world, the males may use the same signals that are meant to attract females to warn off male rivals.

**DELAYED REACTION**
Many snakes can delay egg fertilization, in some cases for months after they have mated. If the old woman of the British nursery rhyme "who had so many children she didn't know what to do" had had the same ability, perhaps her shoe wouldn't have been so crowded.

**FLASHY**
The male frigate bird attracts his mate in very much the same way the anole lizard does. He keeps his pouch inflated for several hours until she succumbs to his charms.

**A COUPLE OF SWELLS**
Anole lizards are highly territorial. The males display regularly to one another, inflating their brilliant reddish throat sacs as a sign of aggression. Two lizards of the same size may flaunt this brightly colored flap of skin at one another for hours at a time, though a smaller lizard will retreat immediately if threatened in this way. Anole lizards come from the tropical areas of South and Central America. They are sometimes called "American chameleons," though they are actually iguanas. They blend in well with the green and brown vegetation in which they live. This helps to protect them from their enemies.

**SPRING IN THE AIR**
Giant tortoises mate in the spring, when the male will often ram the female in the side with his shell to show his interest. The act of mating sometimes takes several hours.

**SNAKE CHARMERS**
Once a male snake has successfully found a female, he approaches her, then stimulates her into mating by rubbing his chin along her back, while their bodies and tails intertwine. During the mating season, two male snakes will sometimes perform a kind of combat dance, as they vie for a particularly favored female. As they wave their bodies around, often hardly touching each other, they have the opportunity to show who is the bigger and stronger animal. The smaller snake may often be frightened away by this behavior.

**MAY THE BEST MAN WIN**
At the beginning of the mating season male monitors wrestle, rearing up on their hind legs. The weaker animal finally gives up, usually before it is injured.

*Tails intertwined during mating*

*Throat sac inflated to attract female or as a sign of aggression*

# Examining eggs

YOUNG REPTILES develop inside an egg, cushioned in a bag of fluid called the amnion. The eggs of most reptiles have a soft and flexible shell, although some have hard shells like birds' eggs. A yolk provides the animal with food, and oxygen and moisture, also necessary for the young reptile's growth and development, are absorbed through the shell. Some lizards and snakes are viviparous, that is, they give birth to fully developed young.

**FACT OR FICTION?**
In Greek mythology there are many tales about a tribe of warlike women, called the Amazons, who hated men and lived without them. Some all-female lizards, like the little whiptail, can reproduce without mating. This is called parthenogenesis.

## Snakes

The eggs of most snakes have a flexible leathery shell. The young snakes hatch by slashing a hole in the shell using a special, sharp egg tooth. Most snakes bury their eggs in a little soil or rotting vegetation. Several vipers, boas, and sea snakes are viviparous.

Ground python egg

Indian python egg

**UNDERGROUND COVER**
Scarcely recognizable as an egg, this extraordinary-looking object was laid by a ground python, a burrowing snake from West Africa. The egg is large in proportion to the mother. A female of 33 in (85 cm) may lay eggs 5 in (12 cm) in length.

**MOTHER LOVE**
After laying about 30 of these leathery-sh eggs, the female Indian python takes unu care of her precious brood, coiling hers around her eggs. By continuously twitch her muscles (much like shivering) she ra the temperature within the coils sever degrees higher than her surroundings

**COMMON AS MUCK**
The common African house snake often c manure heaps or termite mounds in wh lay its eggs, usually eight or ten at a ti

African house snake egg

Whiptail lizard

Monitor lizard egg

## Lizards

Most lizards produce eggs with leathery shells. Lizards are rarely attentive to their eggs once they have been laid. Some skinks, however, return to their nests to brood, raising the temperature of the eggs with their bodies, which have been warmed by the sun.

African chameleon eggs

Javan bloodsucker egg

Tokay gecko eggs

**STUCK ON YOU**
The tokay gecko, like many geckos and skinks, lays eggs two at a time. The eggs are soft and sticky at first, but they harden after being exposed to the air. As the eggs dry, they stick to the surface on which they were laid.

**BURIED ALIVE**
Some chameleons give birth to live young; others lay eggs. The African chameleon, which lives in trees, comes down to the ground to lay its clutch of 30 – 40 eggs in a burrow. The chameleon fills in the burrow to protect the eggs; when the young hatch, they have to dig themselves out.

**SPINDLE EGGS**
The eggs of the tree-dwelling Javan bloodsucker, an agamid lizard, are a most peculiar spindle shape. It is not clear why this is – closely related species have eggs that are more oval in shape.

**CUCKOOS IN THE**
The Nile monitor likes to lay her egg termite mounds. S tears a hole in the the mound and the 40 – 60 eggs. The h inside the mound to incubate the egg which hatch after ten months.

# rocodilians

mans and alligators
d mounds out of
h vegetation, soil, and
litter to nest their
d-shelled eggs;
odiles and gavials
holes for their eggs
xposed beaches and
, crumbly soil. The
ale often stays close
he nest to stop would-
hieves from raiding
ll crocodilian eggs
e to be kept warm. In
, the sex of the
chling is determined
tiny temperature
nges during the early
ges of incubation.

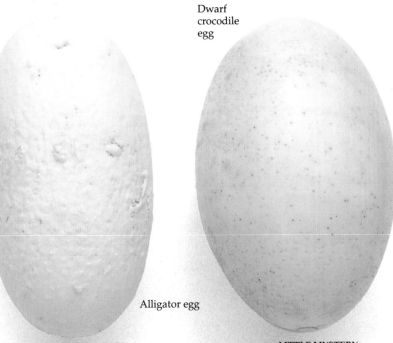

Dwarf
crocodile
egg

Alligator egg

### LENDING A PAW
The female American alligator builds a mound of plant
matter and soil, then digs a hole in it to lay 35 – 40
eggs. When the eggs have hatched and the young
alligators are ready to leave the nest, they grunt loudly
and their mother tears open the nest.

### LITTLE MYSTERY
The African dwarf crocodile is basically
nocturnal. It lays fewer eggs than most
other crocodiles – less than 20 – but they
are quite large and are laid directly into
a specially constructed mound.

### WHO'S EATING WHOM?
Humans and crocodiles live
side by side along the coast
of Papua New Guinea. This
shield shows a figure inside
the crocodile's belly. The
people of Papua New
Guinea believed that
crocodiles held magical
powers.

# rtles and tortoises

toises, and some turtles, lay hard-
lled eggs, but the eggshells of
rine and some river turtles are
. Most females make a hole in the
und for their eggs, and they may
rn to the same spot year after year.
with crocodiles, the sex of baby
tles and tortoises is often deter-
ned by the temperature during
ubation.

Spur-thighed
tortoise egg

Snake-necked
turtle egg

Matamata
egg

### MATAMATA
The eggs of this strange
South American turtle
look very much like Ping-
Pong balls. Like all aquatic
turtles, the matamata must
leave the water to lay her
eggs. These turtles were
previously hunted for their
meat, but they are now
protected by law.

### MEDITERRANEAN
MATES
The spur-thighed tortoise is found
all around the Mediterranean. Up
until recently it was exported in
large numbers to pet shops in
northern European countries. Few
of them survived this experience.
Importing them is now against the
law in many countries.

### SNAKE-NECKED
TURTLE
The Australian snake-
necked turtle leaves
the water to lay her
eggs in a nest that she
digs on dry land. She
lays her eggs at night,
after rainfall.

Galapagos
tortoise egg

### GENTLE GIANT
he Galapagos giant tortoise is one of the
iggest in the world. It lays its hard-shelled
ggs in soil that is exposed to the sun. The
ggs sometimes incubate (develop) for 200
ys. Unfortunately, many are destroyed by
foraging rats and pigs, which were
introduced to the islands by humans.

**MASS NESTING**
Every year some 200,000 Ridley sea turtles come
to Orissa, India, to nest along just 3 miles (5 km)
of beach. Each female digs a hole in which she
lays about 100 eggs, then she returns to the sea.

**ADDED PROTECTION**
Like birds' eggs, rep-
tilian eggs have a
shell which protects
the developing
young, but also
allows it to breathe.
The shell is made up
of several layers. Here
the brittle outer layer has
been broken, revealing a
flexible inner layer. Under
this is the amniotic mem-
brane, which fills with
fluid, creating a suitable
environment for the
developing reptile.

Shell allows
embryo to
breathe

Embryo

Amnion

Yolk
sac

# Spitting images

Baby reptiles are born looking like small versions of their parents. Whether they hatch from eggs (pp. 20–21) or are born live, young reptiles are able to feed themselves and can live in much the same environment as they will when they are fully grown. This is fortunate because most reptiles lay their eggs and then move on, leaving the hatchlings to fend for themselves. There are some exceptions. Some lizards and snakes protect their eggs (p. 21), and some watch their young for a period of a few weeks to two years after hatching. A young reptile's eating habits are not the same as its parents'. As the young animal develops, its growing body demands more food. A young crocodile, for example, may be able to survive on insects, but as it grows bigger, it will eat considerably larger prey, including mammals, birds, and fish.

Caiman

**LIKE MOTHER LIKE DAUGHTER**
This young caiman is born fully formed and able to fend for itself. Like the young alligator, it will stay close to its mother for a few weeks, sometimes using her back as a basking platform. In addition to the mother's protection, unusual in reptiles, the young are able to dive under water for cover at the first sign of danger.

**HATCHING**
The incubation time – the length of time after an egg is laid and before it hatches – for a snake egg, varies according to the temperature. The warmer it is, the faster the eggs develop, so the parent often chooses to lay them in a place that is both warm and slightly moist. Piles of vegetation produce heat as the plant material rots, so compost heaps are sometimes selected as nesting sites, particularly by snakes living in cooler areas. Once they are laid, snake eggs often swell as they absorb moisture from the environment (pp. 20–21). Often the young snake that emerges is much longer than the egg from which it hatched. This is possible because as the embryo develops, the whole body is coiled into a tight spiral.

**1 THE EGG**
This is the egg of a rat snake, a large sna[ke] common in North America. Its mating seaso[n] from April to June. Between June and Augus[t] the female lays 5–30 soft-shelled, oblong egg[s] often choosing rotten wood, leaf litter, or a s[p] under some rocks as her "nest."

**4 MAKING A MOVE**
Once it is ready, the snake leaves the egg quickly. It is able to slither along in the normal snake-like way immediately (pp. 52–53). Interestingly, though, if a snake is removed from its egg a little too early, it will writhe about, unable to move properly. However, in every other way it looks normal. It therefore seems likely that the snake only becomes fully coordinated just before hatching.

**BIG BABIES**
The young of the adder, Britain's only venomous snake, are incredibly large compared with the eggs in which they develop (pp. 20–21).

## LOOKS CAN DECEIVE

Most geckos lay their eggs between pieces of bark or stick them to a wall. This sandstone gecko laid her eggs between the crevices of rocks. The eggs have hard shells that protect them from the wind and rain (pp. 20-21). Although many geckos lay their eggs in a common area, they do not take care of their young – in fact, it is unusual that mother and young should be as close to one another as this. The young are independent from birth, but are not sexually mature, that is, able to reproduce, for about 18 months.

Female

Young

### THE HAZARDS OF HATCHING

Of all the reptiles, turtles lay the most eggs, but care for them the least. Abandoned to the earth or sand in which its egg was buried, this little hatchling will have to fight alone to survive in a dangerous world.

*The young snake checks its surroundings with its tongue*

*The snake is in no hurry to leave the safety of its shell*

## 2 BREAKING THE SHELL

While it is developing inside the egg, the young rat snake takes nourishment from the yolk. A day or two before hatching, the yolk sac is drawn into the body and the remaining yolk is absorbed into the young snake's intestine. A small scar, much like a belly button, shows the point where the embryo was joined to its food supply. As the young snake develops, a sharp but temporary egg tooth grows from the tip of its upper jaw. The hatchling uses this tooth to pierce the eggshell. The young snake gets its first view of the world through one of the slits it makes.

## 3 LEAVING THE EGG

Having tested its surroundings by flicking its tongue in and out (pp. 16–17), the hatchling cautiously emerges from its shell. It is in no hurry to leave, and may stay where it is, with only its head poking out, for a day or two. That way, if disturbed, the young snake can always go back inside the egg. Rat snakes are usually ready to leave their eggs 7–15 weeks after being laid.

## 5 MINOR MIRACLE

It seems amazing that such a long snake could ever have been packed inside such a relatively small egg. The hatchlings may be as much as seven times longer than the egg, or 11–16 in (28–40 cm).

# Scale tale

REPTILES HAVE DRY, SCALY SKINS. As in other creatures, the skin forms a barrier between the animal's tissues and the world outside, protecting it from ordinary wear and tear, from drying out, and from damage by predators. The reptiles' scales are thickenings of this outside layer of skin, and are mostly made of a horny substance called keratin, much like fingernails. The outer skin is shed, or molted, from time to time and then renewed by cells in the inner layer. Molting allows room for growth and at the same time replaces worn-out skin. Lizards and snakes have a characteristic molting, or "sloughing," time which varies from species to species. Most lizards shed their skin in large flakes, often over a few days; snakes slough the entire skin at one time.

*Old skin is fragile and can break easily*

## Skin deep

Reptilian skin varies greatly from one species to another. It may be rough, bumpy, or spiny, as on the tails of certain lizards. Or it may form crests on the neck, back, or tail. In most snakes, the belly scales form a series of wide overlapping plates, which help the snakes when moving (pp. 52–53).

**COUNTING THE SCALES**
The pattern of scales on different parts of the head and body are valuable in helping specialists to identify reptiles. For example, the number of rows of scales at the midbody line and the number of large belly scales are helpful clues to identifying snakes.

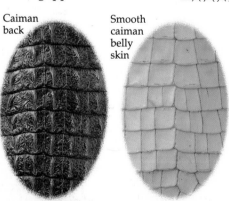

Caiman back

Smooth caiman belly skin

**HORNY-SKINNED**
The caiman's "armor" is made of rough horny scales, or scutes, along the back and tail. The back scales are strengthened by bony plates.

**ON THE CREST**
The scales on the back of the chameleon rise to a crest of points along its length.

**DIGGERS**
The scales of skinks are smooth, so that mud does not cling.

**PLATED LIZARD**
Like the caiman, th[e] lizard has bony pla[tes] under its scales.

*New skin is smooth and shiny*

**RENEWING THE RATTLE**
The tail of the rattlesnake is made up of a series of hollow pieces of keratin locked together. Every time the snake sheds its skin, a new segment is added to the rattle. To warn away its enemies, the snake shakes the rattle by vibrating its tail, and the separate pieces knock together to produce the rattle sound. It is a simple, but effective, device.

**SLOUGHING**
About four times a year, the slowworm sheds its skin in very large pieces. Although it looks like a snake, it is in fact a legless lizard from Europe. Adult lizards molt about once every month when they are most active. Some lizards peel off their old skin in strips with their mouth and swallow the pieces, but the slowworm sheds its old skin more like a snake. The need to molt continues throughout life, because most reptiles never stop growing, though the growth rate is almost undetectable when they are old.

**SHARP DRESSING**
When a cat sharpens its claws, it is also getting rid of dead tissue. People also shed the dead outer layer of their skin, though they only lose little pieces at a time. Humans need to "shed" their clothes regularly as they grow up, much like a snake needs a new, larger skin. Clothes offer protection from the world around us, as our skin is not as efficient as a reptile's.

**ALL IN THE EYE**
Several days before a snake is ready to shed its skin, its eyes look cloudy. Its skin appears dull and colorless, it loses its appetite, and may become aggressive. Many snakes also look for water, as they lose a considerable amount of body fluids along with their skins.

**W SKIN FOR OLD**
akes are able to crawl
t of their old skin, usually
ving it behind in one piece.
ey can do this because they
ve no limbs, which might hinder
e shedding, and because their
ter skin comes off as an all-in-one
it. The sloughing starts along the
s. The snake rubs the side of its
ad along the ground to turn the
in back; it then crawls out of its
in, turning it inside out as it does
Often in no more than half an
ur the snake emerges, shiny and
stening, in its new colors and scales.

Top

Adult rat snake skin

Young rat snake skin

Underside

Young snakes shed soon after they hatch and then about seven times in their first year

# Selection of snakes

ALTHOUGH SNAKES HAVE NO LEGS, eyelids, or eardrums, they can still move quickly and sense their surroundings with special touch and chemical sensors. Snakes are found in many habitats on all continents except Antarctica. Most snakes live on land but some burrow; others live in rivers or the sea, and many climb trees. There are about 2,500 different species. Over 800 of them are poisonous, but only about 250 are considered dangerous to humans.

**BOTTOMS UP**
When threatened, this harmless, long-nosed snake uses an effective, defensive trick. It hides its head under its coiled body, waves its tail in the air, and shoots blood-stained liquid from its anal opening. It lives in prairies and deserts in the U.S. and Mexico and uses its pointed snout to burrow.

**BACK BITER**
This mildly venomous, rear-fanged Madagascan hognose snake rarely bites people. It feeds on small mammals and amphibians, but if it is threatened, it will flatten its neck (like a cobra) and hiss loudly. It shelters in burrows in grassland areas on the island of Madagascar, and grows up to 5 ft (152 cm) long.

**NIGHT-TIME PROWLER**
Another snake harmless to people is the California mountain kingsnake. It is also one of the most colorful snakes found in North America. When the weather is warm, this snake rests during the day and hunts at night for lizards, other snakes, and young birds. It is 40 in (102 cm) long and is found from northern California to southern Washington State.

**CHECKMATE**
This non-poisonous snake from the eastern U.S. is called the corn snake because the checked markings on its underside look like the pattern of kernals on an ear of corn. The longest on record measured 6 ft (183 cm).

**SHRINKING VIOLET**
This shy, gray-banded kingsnake is rarely seen in the wild. Despite its secretive habits, this harmless snake is a popular pet and has bred successfully in captivity. It is 4 ft (121 cm) when fully grown, and lives on a diet of lizards.

**STONY LOOK**
Medusa was a terrifying mythical being. Her head was covered with writhing snakes, and anyone unlucky enough to glance at her would instantly turn to stone.

**BEGONE!**
Legend has it that Ireland has no snakes because St. Patrick banished them to rid the country of evil.

**IN THE BEGINNING**
Snakes have not been very po-
r since the time of the Garden
len, when the devil, in the form
serpent, tempted Eve with the
forbidden fruit. This painting
of that scene, by
Albrecht
Dürer,
was
painted
in 1504.

**STOCK-STILL**
The vine
snake from
Southeast
Asia
spends
hours
hanging
in a tree,
motionless.
Because it
is bright
green and
very slender,
it is well hidden.
Its eyes face
forward, giving it
binocular vision. As a
result, it is good at judging
distances, especially when
lunging at passing lizards.

**DOUBLE BLUFF**
This harmless Sinaloan milk snake,
looks very like the highly venomous
coral snake, which probably deters
quite a few predators from
trying to make a meal of
the snake. Milk snakes
are so-called
because of a
mistaken belief
that they steal
milk from
cows.

**PITS**
copperhead is a North
erican member of the pit
er family. Like its relatives
rattlesnakes, the copperhead
inflict a nasty bite, its
om entering the victim's
dstream, causing internal
ding. However, people
ly die from copperhead
. These snakes grow to
t 3 ft (91 cm).

*Eye facing forward*

**HIGH FLIER**
The flying snake is an energetic, fast-moving tree snake from
southern Asia. It is active by day and hangs high up in the
trees of thick forests hunting for lizards and the occasional
frog. It jumps from branch to branch and even glides through
the air to lower levels. When it wants to slow down, it
flattens its body to increase air resistance.

27

# Loads of lizards

**MEEK AND MILD**
In spite of its fierce appearance, the spiky moloch is harmless. It lives almost exclusively on ants. In addition to giving predators a prickly mouthful, the moloch's spikes have another use: dew condenses on them and runs into the lizard's mouth. In this way, the lizard can live for weeks without drinking.

THERE ARE OVER 3,000 SPECIES OF LIZARD. They form the most successful of all the reptilian groups, having evolved many different life-styles. Although most of them live on the ground, many live in trees, some burrow, and still more live in water. Some lizards have no limbs and are very snake-like. Others can parachute or fly. Geckos, iguanas, chameleons, skinks, and monitors are just a few of the lizards alive today.

**PUNK IS ALIVE**
The common iguana's crest, running like the teeth of a comb down the center of the lizard's back, makes it easy to spot. These lizards are often seen basking in trees.

**BLUE MOVER**
The blue-tongued skink is so-called because of its blue tongue, which it constantly flicks in and out. This skink gives birth to live young. And despite its clumsy appearance it can move fast when necessary.

**KOMODO KING**
The Komodo dragon, a monitor lizard, is the largest living lizard in the world. One captured specimen was 10 ft 2 in (3.10 m) in length and weighed a staggering 365 lb (165.6 kg). The dragon is found only on a few Indonesian islands.

**ARMOR-PLATED**
Plated lizards have tough, bony plates underlying their scales. These lizards normally have long tails but this one has clearly had a narrow escape and its tail has not yet regrown fully (pp. 24–25).

**FLAT AS A PANCAKE**
This African lizard, like many of its family, has a flat body and thick protective scales, and it can slip easily into cracks in boulders. When threatened by a predator, it can jam itself into a crevice where it inflates its body, so that it is very difficult to pry out.

**BLINKING GECKOS**
Leopard geckos are unusual in that they have movable eyelids. Most geckos, like snakes, cannot blink, but have a fixed, transparent window protecting their eyes. Their toes end in tiny pads with many hairlike projections, which can cling to smooth surfaces.

**COLOR CONSCIOUS**
Chameleons generally lead calm lives, which is fortunate, as aside from their ability to change color, they have few defenses against enemies. The male Jackson's chameleon is better off than most – his prehistoric-looking, three-pronged horns probably frighten away many foes.

**TREE CREEPER**
The glossy-skinned, emerald tree skink rarely ventures onto the ground, and spends most of its life scuttling amid the branches of trees in Indonesia.

Emerald tree skink

**A TOE-TO-TAIL TALE**
Chameleons have truly remarkable toes, specialized for life in trees. The toes are arranged so that the feet are able to clasp branches securely. The tail offers extra support, twisting and twining itself around any handy branch. This Madagascan chameleon, like many others, also boasts a strange, sticky-tipped tongue which it can shoot out farther than the length of its body, guaranteeing it a good diet of insects and other small invertebrates.

**OD
LUENCE**
hinese art, common rd has evolved a magnificent gon. The dragon hinese folklore is symbol of rebirth fertility. Because it is ght to be a gentle ture spreading ppiness, it plays a large art in the famous street festivals of many Chinese communities.

*Strong tail aids posture and balance*

**EYED LIZARD**
The eyed or ocellated lizard is only found in Europe and North Africa. It is one of Europe's largest lizards, sometimes growing to a length of 2 ft 7 in (80 cm). This shy lizard is really a ground dweller but can climb well.

# Turtles and tortoises

CHELONIANS, OR REPTILES WITH SHELLS, are found in warm or hot climates in most parts of the world. There are between 250 and 300 species. The shell protects the reptile from knocks and bumps, poor weather conditions, and predators. It is also good camouflage. Chelonians live in salt water, fresh water, and on land. Marine chelonians are called turtles and the rest are tortoises, but sometimes pond and river dwellers are known as terrapins. All chelonians lay eggs on land in a variety of different habitats. Some lay in sand, some in leaf litter, and some in the burrows of other animals. The number of eggs laid varies with the body size of the mother. The smaller species lay one to four eggs per clutch, whereas some large sea turtles regularly lay over 100 eggs at a time.

**TURTLE GOD**
In Brahmin mythology, after one of the great floods, the god Vishnu returned to earth as the turtle Kurma. He came to help rescue the world.

**GALAPAGOS GIANTS**
Charles Darwin wrote about th
Galapagos Islands of the Pacifi
Ocean in 1835. He found the gi
tortoises had adapted to life on
own island. There are two mai
groups: the saddlebacks, which
reach up to tall vegetation for f
food, and the domeshells, whic
graze on the ground.

**LONESOME GEORGE**
On the island of Santa Cruz in the Galapagos Islands, a giant tortoise, nearly 3 ft (1 m) in length, lives alone. He appears to be the last remaining giant tortoise from neighboring Pinta Island. Many attempts have been made to find a female from the same island, but without success. It seems George will live and die alone.

**HALF AND HALF**
Pond terrapins are mainly vegetarian and spend most of their time in water, though they do come onto land to bask. The lungs of some of the pond terrapins of southern Asia are enclosed in bony boxes formed by the inner walls of the shell. This box protects the lungs from increased pressure when the animals dive to great depths. The European pond terrapin is found throughout Europe, western Asia, and northwest Africa. It is a shy creature and dives into the water when approached.

*The car*
*covers the*

*The plastron covers the belly*

The shell is made up of 59 to 61 bones and is in two parts, the plastron and the carapace

The red or yellow "ear marking" makes this turtle instantly recognizable

**RED EARS**
Red-eared terrapins got their name because of the broad, red stripe that runs along the side of the head. Because they are gentle and attractive creatures they are very popular as pets. Unfortunately, they seldom reach maturity in captivity because they do not receive the vitamins and minerals they need. They live in ponds and rivers in the U.S., but frequently climb out of the water to bask, often on logs, where they may pile up several deep.

The plastron and carapace are joined on each side by a girdle bone

**LETHAL SOFTY**
The shell of soft-shelled turtles has no horny plates and feels like leather. In Africa, Asia, Indonesia, and North America they are usually found buried in mud in rivers and ponds, though like many other turtles they enjoy basking in the sun. They are able to breathe while in the water by stretching their long necks to the surface and taking a breath through the snorkel-like nose. They hide from enemies but are fierce and effective hunters and can strike at lightning speed.

**RECORD REPTILE**
The leatherback is the largest of all living turtles, and according to some records, it is also the heaviest. In 1988 this enormous leatherback drowned when it became entangled in fishermen's line. It was washed up in Harlech Bay in Wales. It weighed 2,016 lb (752 kg), and is the biggest turtle ever recorded. These turtles breed in the Caribbean, then follow jellyfish, their main food, across the Atlantic.

Hawksbill turtle shell

Large scales, called scutes, cover the bone of the shell

Starred tortoise shell

Radiated tortoise shell

**SHELLS**
Different life-styles lead to alterations in shell structure. Tortoises usually have high-domed or knobby shells as protection against a predator's strong jaws. Turtles tend to have flatter shells, which are streamlined for easy movement through the water. The soft-shelled turtles have the flattest shells, which allow them to hide easily beneath sand and mud.

# Turtle tank

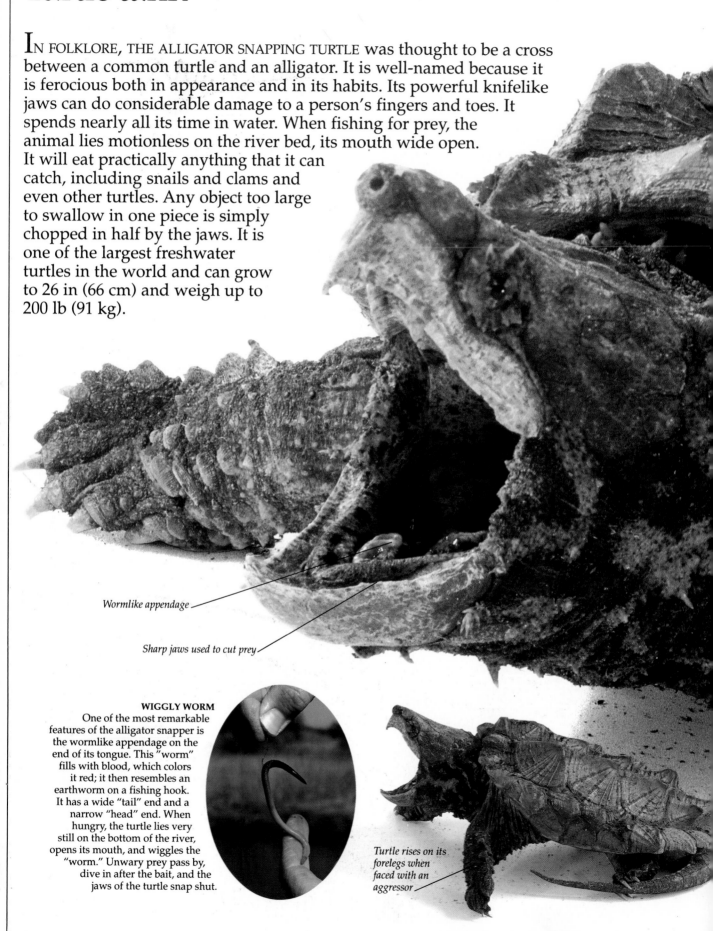

IN FOLKLORE, THE ALLIGATOR SNAPPING TURTLE was thought to be a cross between a common turtle and an alligator. It is well-named because it is ferocious both in appearance and in its habits. Its powerful knifelike jaws can do considerable damage to a person's fingers and toes. It spends nearly all its time in water. When fishing for prey, the animal lies motionless on the river bed, its mouth wide open. It will eat practically anything that it can catch, including snails and clams and even other turtles. Any object too large to swallow in one piece is simply chopped in half by the jaws. It is one of the largest freshwater turtles in the world and can grow to 26 in (66 cm) and weigh up to 200 lb (91 kg).

*Wormlike appendage*

*Sharp jaws used to cut prey*

**WIGGLY WORM**
One of the most remarkable features of the alligator snapper is the wormlike appendage on the end of its tongue. This "worm" fills with blood, which colors it red; it then resembles an earthworm on a fishing hook. It has a wide "tail" end and a narrow "head" end. When hungry, the turtle lies very still on the bottom of the river, opens its mouth, and wiggles the "worm." Unwary prey pass by, dive in after the bait, and the jaws of the turtle snap shut.

*Turtle rises on its forelegs when faced with an aggressor*

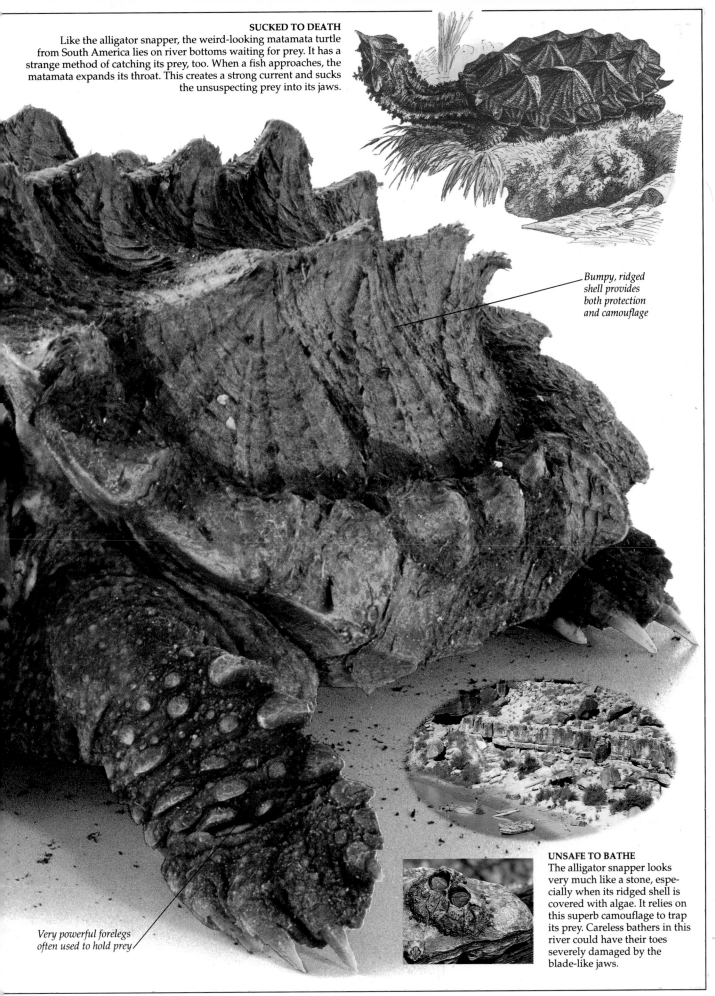

Like the alligator snapper, the weird-looking matamata turtle from South America lies on river bottoms waiting for prey. It has a strange method of catching its prey, too. When a fish approaches, the matamata expands its throat. This creates a strong current and sucks the unsuspecting prey into its jaws.

*Bumpy, ridged shell provides both protection and camouflage*

*Very powerful forelegs often used to hold prey*

**UNSAFE TO BATHE**
The alligator snapper looks very much like a stone, especially when its ridged shell is covered with algae. It relies on this superb camouflage to trap its prey. Careless bathers in this river could have their toes severely damaged by the blade-like jaws.

33

# The crocodile clan

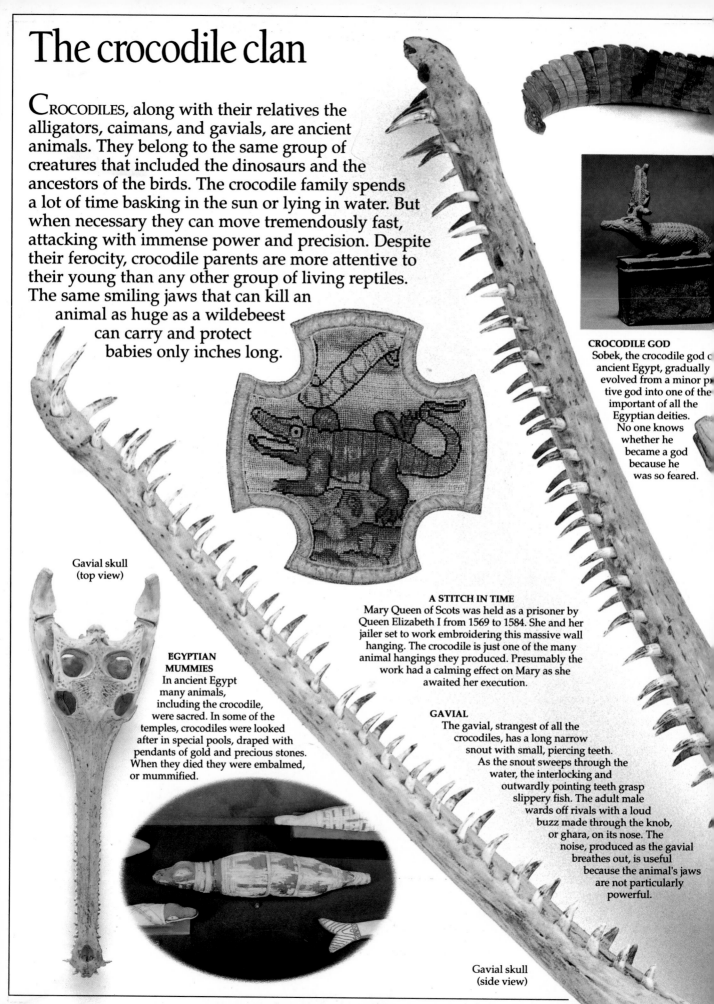

CROCODILES, along with their relatives the alligators, caimans, and gavials, are ancient animals. They belong to the same group of creatures that included the dinosaurs and the ancestors of the birds. The crocodile family spends a lot of time basking in the sun or lying in water. But when necessary they can move tremendously fast, attacking with immense power and precision. Despite their ferocity, crocodile parents are more attentive to their young than any other group of living reptiles. The same smiling jaws that can kill an animal as huge as a wildebeest can carry and protect babies only inches long.

**CROCODILE GOD**
Sobek, the crocodile god of ancient Egypt, gradually evolved from a minor pri tive god into one of the important of all the Egyptian deities. No one knows whether he became a god because he was so feared.

Gavial skull
(top view)

**EGYPTIAN MUMMIES**
In ancient Egypt many animals, including the crocodile, were sacred. In some of the temples, crocodiles were looked after in special pools, draped with pendants of gold and precious stones. When they died they were embalmed, or mummified.

**A STITCH IN TIME**
Mary Queen of Scots was held as a prisoner by Queen Elizabeth I from 1569 to 1584. She and her jailer set to work embroidering this massive wall hanging. The crocodile is just one of the many animal hangings they produced. Presumably the work had a calming effect on Mary as she awaited her execution.

**GAVIAL**
The gavial, strangest of all the crocodiles, has a long narrow snout with small, piercing teeth. As the snout sweeps through the water, the interlocking and outwardly pointing teeth grasp slippery fish. The adult male wards off rivals with a loud buzz made through the knob, or ghara, on its nose. The noise, produced as the gavial breathes out, is useful because the animal's jaws are not particularly powerful.

Gavial skull
(side view)

Caiman

Caiman skull
(side view)

Caiman skull
(top view)

**CAIMAN**

Caimans are members of the alligator family. Their snouts are rather short and broad, and, as with alligators, the teeth on the lower jaw are largely invisible when the mouth is closed. Young caimans eat mainly insects, but as they grow, their diet grows too, to include water snails, fish, mammals, and birds. One species of broad-snouted caiman is particularly adaptable and has been seen in cattle ponds and in heavily polluted rivers near large cities.

*Eye sockets*

Crocodile skull
(side view)

*Prominent tooth*

Crocodile skull
(top view)

**CROCODILE**

In crocodiles some of the teeth on the lower jaw stick out above the upper jaw when the mouth is shut. They are perfect for gripping and puncturing, but are not so good at slicing and chewing. When a crocodile is eating an animal as large as a buffalo, it will seize part of the carcass in its jaws, and roll over and over until a chunk is torn away.

Alligator skull
(side view)

*Lower jaw openings*

**ALLIGATOR**

The American alligator can use its jaws with surprising delicacy. The female, for example, sometimes helps her eggs hatch by lifting them into her mouth, where she gently cracks them open by rolling them against the roof of her mouth with her tongue. The alligator is a massive creature, reaching up to 20 ft (6 m) in length.

Alligator skull
(top view)

*External nostrils*

# The living fossil

THE TUATARA IS CALLED A "LIVING FOSSIL" because it is the sole survivor of an order of reptiles that is otherwise extinct. In fact, it is remarkable that the tuatara has survived, and no one really knows why, since its closest relatives died out millions of years ago. Today, tuataras live on a few small islands off the coast of New Zealand, where they are active at night. They inhabit burrows that are also often occupied by sea birds (pp. 60–61). Although the tuatara looks like a lizard, it differs from lizards in a number of ways. Tuataras have a low metabolic rate (the rate at which food is converted into energy) and are able to function well in much colder temperatures than other reptiles. They also have an extremely slow growth rate and are sometimes still growing at 50–60 years of age.

Male

Female

**KITH OR KIN?**
These are the fossilized remains of *Homoeosaurus*, a tuatara-like animal that lived about 140 million years ago in what is now Europe. "Sphenodontida," the group that contains the tuatara and its fossil relatives, were very widespread and successful animals at that time. It seems likely that the sphenodontids separated from early lizards some 200 million years ago.

*Short, strong legs suitable for excavating burrows*

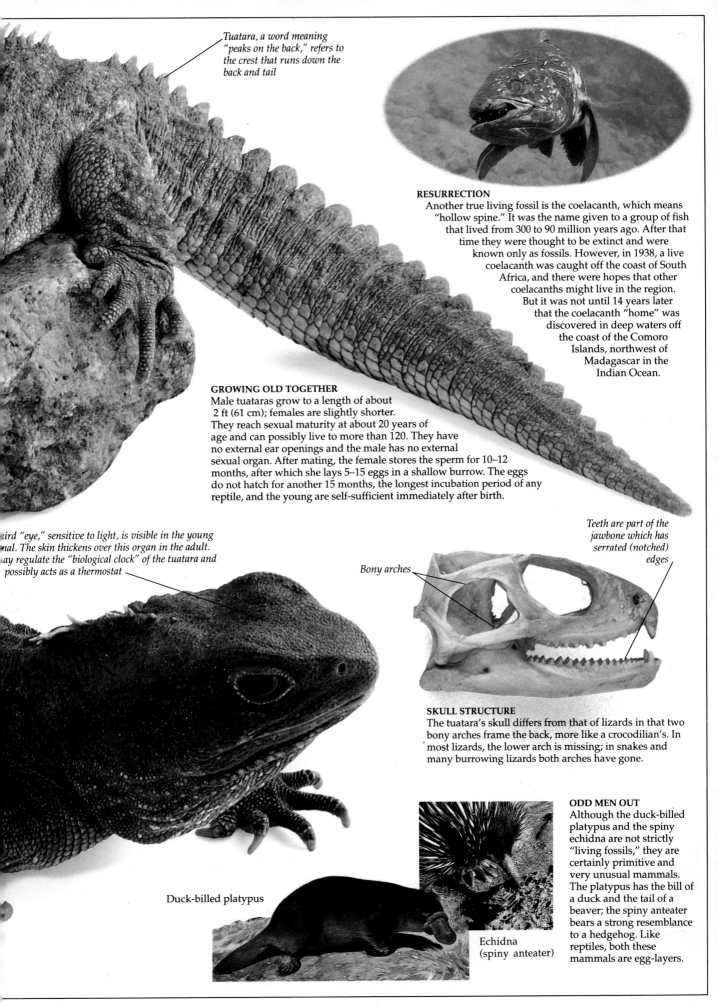

*Tuatara, a word meaning "peaks on the back," refers to the crest that runs down the back and tail*

### RESURRECTION

Another true living fossil is the coelacanth, which means "hollow spine." It was the name given to a group of fish that lived from 300 to 90 million years ago. After that time they were thought to be extinct and were known only as fossils. However, in 1938, a live coelacanth was caught off the coast of South Africa, and there were hopes that other coelacanths might live in the region. But it was not until 14 years later that the coelacanth "home" was discovered in deep waters off the coast of the Comoro Islands, northwest of Madagascar in the Indian Ocean.

### GROWING OLD TOGETHER

Male tuataras grow to a length of about 2 ft (61 cm); females are slightly shorter. They reach sexual maturity at about 20 years of age and can possibly live to more than 120. They have no external ear openings and the male has no external sexual organ. After mating, the female stores the sperm for 10–12 months, after which she lays 5–15 eggs in a shallow burrow. The eggs do not hatch for another 15 months, the longest incubation period of any reptile, and the young are self-sufficient immediately after birth.

*...ird "eye," sensitive to light, is visible in the young ...al. The skin thickens over this organ in the adult. ...ay regulate the "biological clock" of the tuatara and possibly acts as a thermostat*

*Teeth are part of the jawbone which has serrated (notched) edges*

*Bony arches*

### SKULL STRUCTURE

The tuatara's skull differs from that of lizards in that two bony arches frame the back, more like a crocodilian's. In most lizards, the lower arch is missing; in snakes and many burrowing lizards both arches have gone.

### ODD MEN OUT

Although the duck-billed platypus and the spiny echidna are not strictly "living fossils," they are certainly primitive and very unusual mammals. The platypus has the bill of a duck and the tail of a beaver; the spiny anteater bears a strong resemblance to a hedgehog. Like reptiles, both these mammals are egg-layers.

Duck-billed platypus

Echidna (spiny anteater)

# A bite to eat

**SLOW BUT SURE**
Very few tortoises or turtles have the speed or agility to catch fast-moving prey. As a result, most feed on vegetation or on slow-moving animals, such as mollusks, worms, and insect larvae. They all make the most of food that is nearby. The spur-thighed tortoise eats fleshy plants but enjoys the occasional piece of dead animal it finds.

MOST REPTILES ARE MEAT-EATERS, or carnivores. Crocodiles and snakes are all carnivores and have perfected methods of eating their food. Some snakes have specialized diets, such as only birds' eggs (pp. 44–45) or only fish eggs (eaten by some sea snakes). Many lizards are also predators, feeding on insects, mammals, birds, and other reptiles. The Komodo dragon has serrated (notched) teeth much like a shark's, which it uses to cut chunks of flesh from prey as big as water buffalos. Some lizards, however, are mostly vegetarian, including large iguanas, some of the bigger skinks, and a few agamids. Tortoises eat a variety of plants, but even they occasionally eat meat. Terrapins often eat worms, snails, fish, and other small animals. Sea turtles generally feed on jelly-fish, crabs, mollusks, and fish, but they also eat plants. In fact, the green turtle eats little besides sea grass.

**HOOK MEETS HIS END**
In J. M. Barrie's *Peter Pan*, Hook is haunted by the crocodile that has already eaten his hand – and is looking for more! Usually warned of its presence by a clock that ticks in the creature's stomach, Hook is finally tricked.

**CROCODILE LARDER**
Nile crocodiles occasionally share the carcass of a large animal such as a wildebeest or a buffalo. Crocodile stomachs are only the size of a basketball, so crocodiles cannot eat a big animal all at once. Prey is often left in one spot to be finished off later. This has led to the mistaken belief that crocodiles like to eat rotten meat, hiding a freshly killed animal until it is "high," or spoiled. In fact, they prefer fresh meat.

Armlets

Pieces of turtle shell

Stones

Bangle

Porcupine quills

**STOMACH STORE**
Crocodiles often devour hard, heavy objects, such as stones and pieces of metal, possibly to help them digest their food. One can only hope that no one was wearing the bangle when it was swallowed!

Shed tooth    Tooth in use

Developing tooth

**DEVELOPING TEETH**
Mammals grow only two sets of teeth – baby, or "milk" teeth, and then eventually a set of adult teeth. Crocodiles shed their teeth throughout their lives, with new ones constantly replacing old ones. The developing teeth grow up through the holes of those already in use.

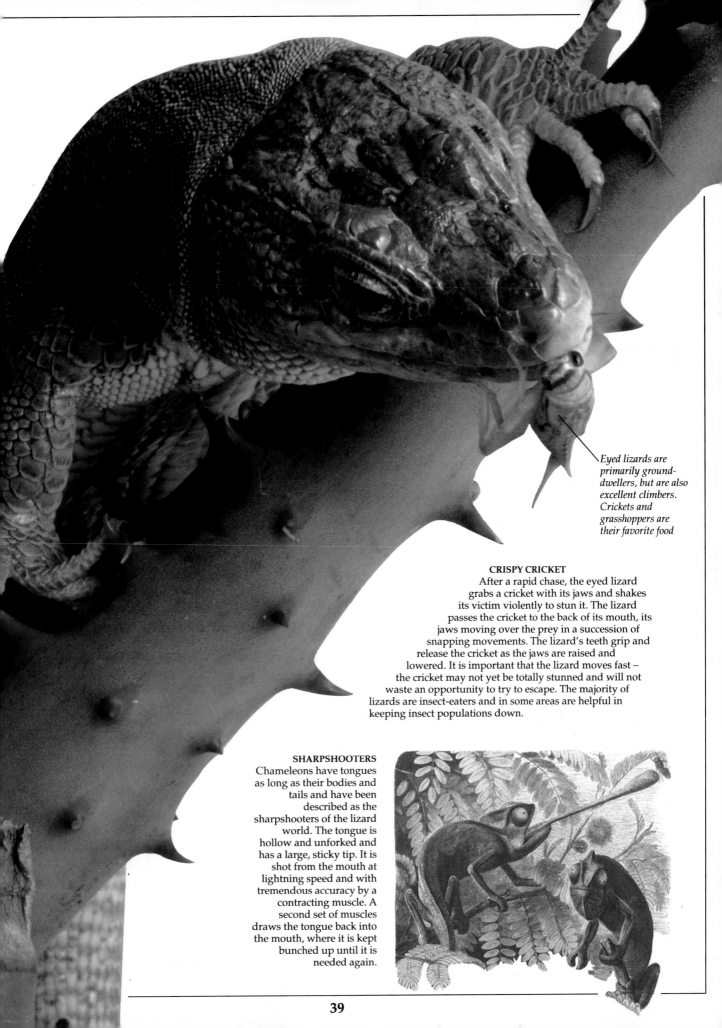

*Eyed lizards are primarily ground-dwellers, but are also excellent climbers. Crickets and grasshoppers are their favorite food*

## CRISPY CRICKET

After a rapid chase, the eyed lizard grabs a cricket with its jaws and shakes its victim violently to stun it. The lizard passes the cricket to the back of its mouth, its jaws moving over the prey in a succession of snapping movements. The lizard's teeth grip and release the cricket as the jaws are raised and lowered. It is important that the lizard moves fast – the cricket may not yet be totally stunned and will not waste an opportunity to try to escape. The majority of lizards are insect-eaters and in some areas are helpful in keeping insect populations down.

## SHARPSHOOTERS

Chameleons have tongues as long as their bodies and tails and have been described as the sharpshooters of the lizard world. The tongue is hollow and unforked and has a large, sticky tip. It is shot from the mouth at lightning speed and with tremendous accuracy by a contracting muscle. A second set of muscles draws the tongue back into the mouth, where it is kept bunched up until it is needed again.

# A tight squeeze

ALL SNAKES EAT MEAT, and they have had to develop many different ways of killing their food. Many snakes kill their prey with venom (pp. 42–43), but boas and pythons kill by squeezing, or constricting, their prey. Constrictors, which eat mainly mammals, do not crush their victims as many people think. The snake coils its body around its struggling victim, making it harder and harder for the prey to breathe, until it finally suffocates. The snake applies just enough pressure to match the breathing movements of its prey. Any mammal, from a mouse to a deer, may become a snake's victim, depending on the size of the snake. In fact, giant snakes can swallow surprisingly big animals. An anaconda over 25 ft (8 m) long can eat a caiman nearly 6 ft (2 m) long, though it may take more than a week to digest.

(pp. 42–43)

**TINTIN TO RESCUE!**
There are a ... Asian and A... records of hu... who have be... killed and eat... some of the la... species of pyt... In one of the ... known *Tintin* books, Zorrino... guide has a luc... escape (contrary... appearances her... saved just in tim... by his friend Tin...

**DANGEROUS ACT**
Circus act performers who dance with constrictors are taking a great risk. This drawing is of a dancer who was nearly suffocated by a python – and was rescued only seconds before certain death.

2 **DEADLY EMBRACE**
The constricting snake reacts to every minute movement of the rat, tightening its grip all the time. ... responds to even the smallest vibrations produced b... the rat's beating heart, and the snake will not release its hold until the beating finally stops. Death comes fairly quickly and bones are rarely broken. The snak... shifts the rat into a good position so that it can be swallowed head first. That way it slips down the throat quite easily.

3 **BIG MOUTH**
The snake's mouth is very flexible. Each bone can move individually – up and down, back and forth, and from side to side – while the backward-pointing teeth grip tightly. As the powerful jaws move over the head of the rat, it looks as though the snake is "walking over" its food.

4 **SAFETY FIRST**
It may take the snake an hour or more to swallow some of its larger victims. The prey is drawn in by the snake's trunk muscles. The snake then forms a sharp curve in its neck behind the prey and pushes it down into the stomach. If, however, the snake is frightened while it is eating, it can regurgitate (spit out) its meal in order to escape swiftly.

5 **TIGHT FIT**
Now, most of the rat has disappeared. The flexible ligament, much like an elastic muscle ... connects the two halves of the snake's lower ja... allows the snake to open its mouth very wide. As the lower jaws are forced apart, the muscle between them stretches to the shape of the prey.

*Body can expand to allow for large prey*

**DINNER TIME**
A snake can usually afford to ignore a prey that could put up a dangerous fight. After an enormous feast – for example, an entire leopard – the snake may not eat again for as much as a year.

**FANGS OF DEATH**
When a hungry boa constrictor attacks its prey, it looks for an end where it can start swallowing – usually the head end. If the victim is wriggly and fat, like this rat, the snake will strike with its long front teeth. Having secured the rat in its jaws, the snake starts to coil around it.

Jaw closed

Jaw open

*Special hinged bone*

**OPEN WIDE**
The jaws of a snake are very flexible, so prey can be swallowed headfirst and whole, even when the victim's body is wider than the snake's. A special bone, linking the lower jaw to the skull, works like a double-jointed hinge. The lower jaw can be stretched sideways, because the two halves are connected at the chin by a flexible ligament that works like an elastic muscle.

**SNAKE EATS SNAKE**
When a California king snake meets a rattlesnake, it grips the rattler with its jaws just behind the head. Then the king snake loops its body around the victim, squeezing until the rattler suffocates.

**WILD CAT STRIKE**
In Kenya, a Thompson's gazelle falls victim to a cheetah. The massive jaws of the cat clamp on to the throat of the struggling prey, possibly causing it to suffocate. But no one really knows whether the gazelle dies by suffocation – in the same way as a boa's prey – or whether it is finished off by the sharp, pointed teeth and powerful claws of the cheetah.

**6 THE END OF THE ROAD**
At this point the snake could face breathing difficulties, but it overcomes the problem by pushing its windpipe forward towards the front of its mouth using it as a built-in "snorkel".

# Name your poison

POISONOUS SNAKES ARE FOUND in many parts of the world in most habitats, but the most poisonous species tend to be concentrated in tropical areas. A snake injects poison, or venom, into its prey, using specially adapted teeth or fangs. In the most dangerous venomous snakes, such as vipers, cobras, and sea snakes, the fangs are found at the front of the upper jaw, but in other snakes they are sometimes at the back. The venom itself is a complicated "cocktail" that affects the prey's nervous system, tissues, or blood – or all three. Its main purpose is to subdue the prey so that the snake can then kill it, but the snake also uses venom to defend itself. However, most snakes will try to avoid a fight, escaping when possible.

*Cheek muscles contract, forcing venom out*

**CRUEL TO BE KIND**
In many parts of the world, people still m[ilk] snakes for their venom, as venom is use[d] produce serum (fluid used in medicine] prevent the action of poison) against snake bites. The snake is held by the back of the head and made to bite through tissue covering the top o[f] small container. It is then forced eject the venom by gentle pressure on the venom sac the cheeks. In time, the animal produces mo[re] venom.

**RATTLESNAKE**
Rattlesnakes are extremely venomous snakes. They are sometimes known as pit vipers because they have a remarkably keen heat-sensitive pit between their nostrils and eyes that enables them to locate prey at night. Even in total darkness, they can detect and strike accurately at objects only a fraction of a degree warmer than their surroundings. A rattlesnake's age cannot be determined by the number of rattles on its tail, as some people believe. In fact, the snake may shed its skin and add a new rattle two or three times a year.

Sea snake

*Venom passes through tube*

*Hole in the tip of the fang*

*Venom sac*

**FANG FACTS**
A rattlesnake's fangs lay against the roof of the mouth until needed, then the upper jaw bone rotates, bringing the fangs forward for biting. Snakes use one pair at a time; one or more spare pairs are arranged in formation behind them.

**OTHER POISONERS**
The sea snake is the most venomous snake in the world. It can swim extremely fast and stay under water for up to five hours. There are two species of poisonous lizard – the Gila monster and the Mexican beaded lizard. Both are found in the southwestern U.S. and in parts of Mexico. Their venom comes from saliva glands in the lower jaw, and the lizards chew it into the victim.

Gila monster

**SOLO SHREW**
The short-tailed shrew is the only mammal with a venomous bite. It has glands in its mouth that produce a nerve poison. When this little creature bites its prey, usually smaller mammals, the venom in the saliva enters the wound and is powerful enough to kill in seconds.

## STAR PERFORMERS

Snakes have appeared in literature for hundreds of years. In Shakespeare's *Antony and Cleopatra*, Cleopatra commited suicide using an asp, a type of cobra commonly found in Egypt and East Africa. The asp's bite is deadly from the moment the snake leaves the shell. Snakes have also starred in films, such as *True Grit*. Here, John Wayne examines Kim Darby's hand after she has been bitten.

Antony and Cleopatra

## SNAKE STONES

Snake stones were once thought to cure snakebites. They were often made of burned bone, chalk, horn, or other absorbent materials, which were believed to "absorb" the venom from a bite when pressed against it.

*Special scales make up rattle*

*Hollow segments which lock together*

Rattle

*Rapid vibration produces a sizzling sound*

# Egg-eating snakes

SOME SNAKES EAT NOTHING but eggs and have become specially adapted for the task. Small eggs, especially the soft-shelled ones laid by lizards and some snakes, are easy to eat, as they can be quickly slit open by the snake's teeth. Larger, hard-shelled eggs, such as those laid by birds, need special treatment. True egg-eating snakes eat only birds' eggs, which they swallow whole. These snakes have few teeth, instead they have toothlike spines on the backbone that crack open the egg as it passes down through the snake's throat.

## Diet of eggs

One problem with an egg diet is that food is not always available. In some parts of the world, birds only lay their eggs at certain times of the year, and so a snake may have to go a long time without food. Fortunately, egg-eating snakes can bring up, or regurgitate, eggshell. This means that no space is wasted in the snake's stomach, and it can eat as many eggs as it finds. It also means the snake does not waste vital energy digesting the shell.

**2 SWALLOW HARD**
The egg is passing down the snake's throat. The skin on the side of the neck is very elastic. At this stage the egg is still unbroken.

*Head arches down, pushing egg against bony inner spines to puncture shell*

*Finely interlinked scales, which separate as skin stretches*

**3 SPINY BONES**
The passage of the egg has now been stopped by the toothlike spines on the underside of the neck bones.

*A valve at the entrance to the stomach accepts yolks and liquids, but rejects pieces of shell*

*The "bulge" is noticeably smaller*

**4 GOING DOWN...**
Once the egg has been punctured, the muscles of the snake's body work in waves to squeeze out the contents, which then continue on to the stomach. The snake now bends its body into S-shaped curves, forcing the collapsed shell back toward the mouth.

**5 AND UP IT COMES...**
It may take from five minutes to an hour for the egg to be completely swallowed, depending on its size. Finally, the snake gapes widely and the compacted cigar-shaped shell is brought up. The fragments of shell are still held together by the sticky egg membranes.

*The jagged edges of the shell pieces are stuck together. All the contents of the egg have been drained*

Regurgitated shell

n African egg-eater is
to swallow an egg. It
impossible – the egg is
the width of the snake's
The snake has a lightly
skull and its mouth is
with sticky ridges.

*Mouth ridges grip the
egg as it passes toward
the snake's throat*

*Because of its shape, an egg is remarkably
resistant to crushing before it is pierced by
the snake's bony spines*

**STOP! THIEF!**
Monitor lizards, which
include some of the
giants of the reptilian
world, are well-
known for their
greed. They feed on
live animals and on
the carcasses of dead
animals. A nest of eggs
is not safe with these
lizards around.

# Survival

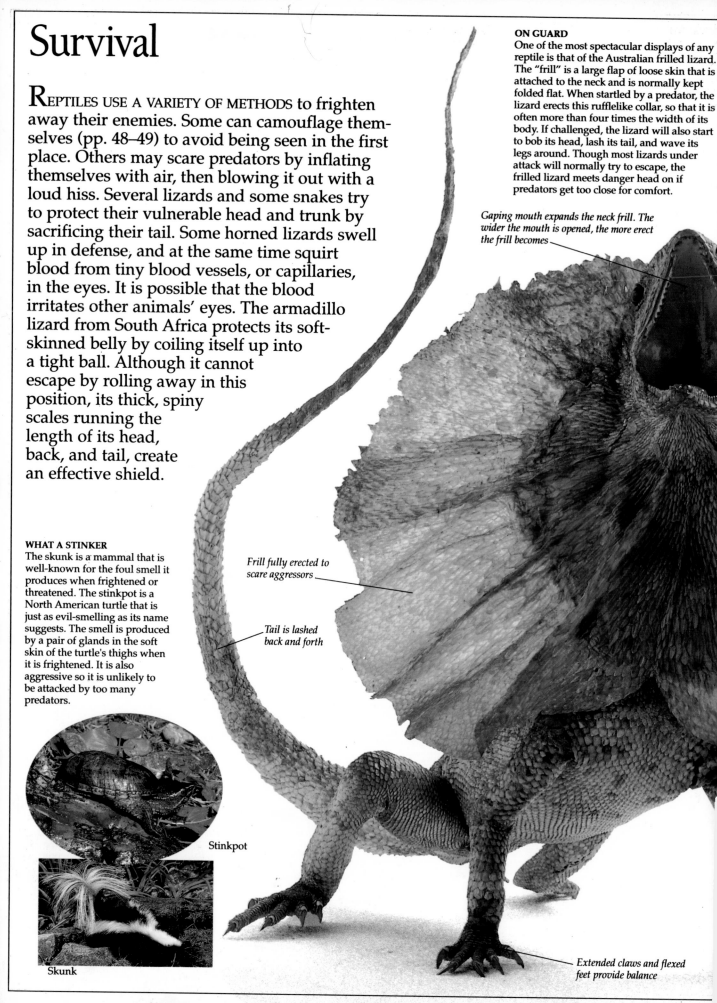

REPTILES USE A VARIETY OF METHODS to frighten away their enemies. Some can camouflage themselves (pp. 48–49) to avoid being seen in the first place. Others may scare predators by inflating themselves with air, then blowing it out with a loud hiss. Several lizards and some snakes try to protect their vulnerable head and trunk by sacrificing their tail. Some horned lizards swell up in defense, and at the same time squirt blood from tiny blood vessels, or capillaries, in the eyes. It is possible that the blood irritates other animals' eyes. The armadillo lizard from South Africa protects its soft-skinned belly by coiling itself up into a tight ball. Although it cannot escape by rolling away in this position, its thick, spiny scales running the length of its head, back, and tail, create an effective shield.

**ON GUARD**
One of the most spectacular displays of any reptile is that of the Australian frilled lizard. The "frill" is a large flap of loose skin that is attached to the neck and is normally kept folded flat. When startled by a predator, the lizard erects this rufflelike collar, so that it is often more than four times the width of its body. If challenged, the lizard will also start to bob its head, lash its tail, and wave its legs around. Though most lizards under attack will normally try to escape, the frilled lizard meets danger head on if predators get too close for comfort.

*Gaping mouth expands the neck frill. The wider the mouth is opened, the more erect the frill becomes*

**WHAT A STINKER**
The skunk is a mammal that is well-known for the foul smell it produces when frightened or threatened. The stinkpot is a North American turtle that is just as evil-smelling as its name suggests. The smell is produced by a pair of glands in the soft skin of the turtle's thighs when it is frightened. It is also aggressive so it is unlikely to be attacked by too many predators.

*Frill fully erected to scare aggressors*

*Tail is lashed back and forth*

Stinkpot

Skunk

*Extended claws and flexed feet provide balance*

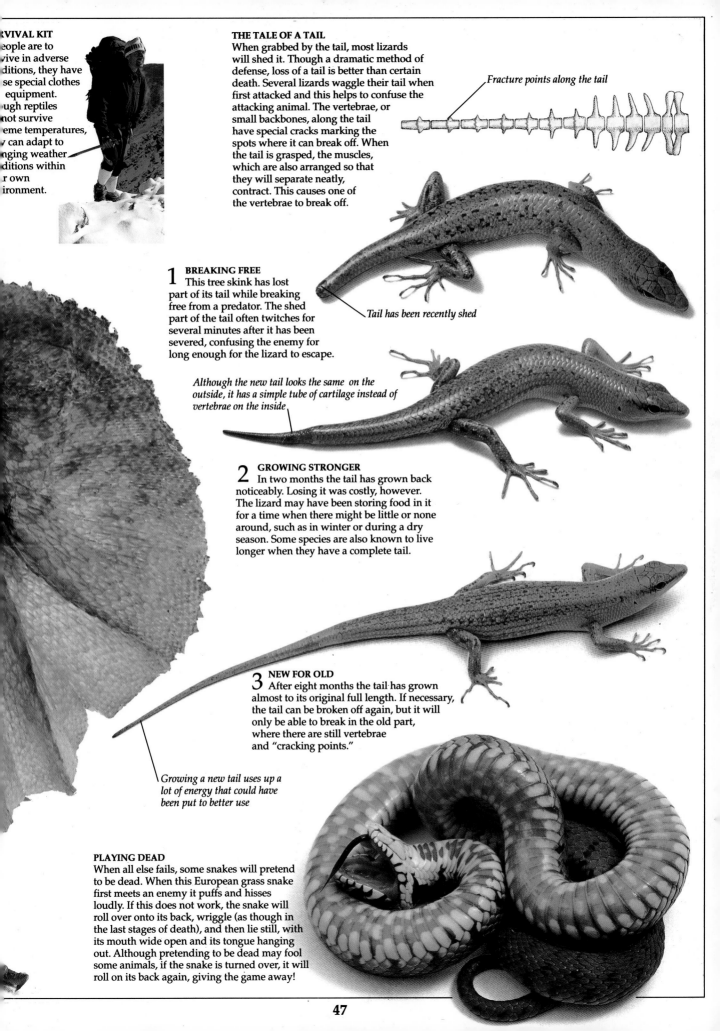

RVIVAL KIT
eople are to
vive in adverse
ditions, they have
se special clothes
equipment.
ugh reptiles
not survive
eme temperatures,
v can adapt to
nging weather
ditions within
r own
ironment.

## THE TALE OF A TAIL

When grabbed by the tail, most lizards
will shed it. Though a dramatic method of
defense, loss of a tail is better than certain
death. Several lizards waggle their tail when
first attacked and this helps to confuse the
attacking animal. The vertebrae, or
small backbones, along the tail
have special cracks marking the
spots where it can break off. When
the tail is grasped, the muscles,
which are also arranged so that
they will separate neatly,
contract. This causes one of
the vertebrae to break off.

*Fracture points along the tail*

### 1 BREAKING FREE

This tree skink has lost
part of its tail while breaking
free from a predator. The shed
part of the tail often twitches for
several minutes after it has been
severed, confusing the enemy for
long enough for the lizard to escape.

*Tail has been recently shed*

*Although the new tail looks the same on the
outside, it has a simple tube of cartilage instead of
vertebrae on the inside*

### 2 GROWING STRONGER

In two months the tail has grown back
noticeably. Losing it was costly, however.
The lizard may have been storing food in it
for a time when there might be little or none
around, such as in winter or during a dry
season. Some species are also known to live
longer when they have a complete tail.

### 3 NEW FOR OLD

After eight months the tail has grown
almost to its original full length. If necessary,
the tail can be broken off again, but it will
only be able to break in the old part,
where there are still vertebrae
and "cracking points."

*Growing a new tail uses up a
lot of energy that could have
been put to better use*

### PLAYING DEAD

When all else fails, some snakes will pretend
to be dead. When this European grass snake
first meets an enemy it puffs and hisses
loudly. If this does not work, the snake will
roll over onto its back, wriggle (as though in
the last stages of death), and then lie still, with
its mouth wide open and its tongue hanging
out. Although pretending to be dead may fool
some animals, if the snake is turned over, it will
roll on its back again, giving the game away!

# Blending in

MANY REPTILES ARE ABLE TO CHANGE their appearance in order to make themselves hard to see against their natural background. This ability, known as camouflage, is used to avoid being spotted by enemies; it is also used to help the reptile ambush unsuspecting prey. Some reptiles are naturally camouflaged, and their skin color matches their background perfectly. In other reptiles, the pattern on the skin helps to break up the outline of the body. In a few, it is the shape of the animal that camouflages it. For example, the fleshy side fringes and leaf-shaped tail of a tree-living gecko, helps it blend almost perfectly with the bark and lichen of the tree trunks it clings to.

**COLOR CONSCIOUS**
Lizards, especially chameleons, are the true masters of camouflage. Many can make the color of their skin lighter or darker as needed. Although these changes take place so that the chameleon can match its background, many other things influence the color change. Light level, temperature, and the mood of the lizard (for example if it is frightened) can all affect the color it takes on.

The chameleon's skin has several layers of color cells. Beneath these are the melanophores, cells with tentacle-like arms that extend through the other layers.

The color change is caused by the melanophores moving a dark brown pigment in and out of the upper layers of the skin.

**FLOWER POWER**
Do not be fooled by this little head. Beneath the leafy canopy is the large bo of the Murray River tu from eastern Australia. I a powerful swimmer and mainly carnivorous, thoug it will eat a few plants.

**LEAF GREEN**
Hard to spot against the palm trees on which they are commonly found, these little tree skinks live in the forests of Indonesia, the Philippines, and the Solomon Islands. The bright green and mottled brown of their bodies, make them almost invisible. Green is understandably a popular color among tree-living reptiles active in the day.

# My Handprint

Trace your hand here. Measure its length and width.

- 3 -

Teaching Aid 8.1b

---

# Some Special Measures

my armspan

_____ cm

length of my shoe _____ cm

my mouth when I'm serious

_____ cm

my mouth in a big grin

_____ cm

- 2 -

# BUTTERFLY NECTAR

Measure into blender:

375 ml milk

1 small banana

1.25 ml cinnamon

4 ice cubes

Whirl mixture until smooth.
Pour into 4 small cups.
Sip "butterfly style" from
a straw "proboscis."

Teaching Aid 8.2a

From Exploring Mathematics: Activities for Concept and Skill Development, Copyright © 1990 Scott, Foresman and Company.

## UBLE TROUBLE

ng still in the leaf litter of the forests of
ical Africa, these gaboon vipers are
rly invisible in the dappled light and
de, as they wait for rodents, frogs, and
ds. Yet when one of the snakes is
oved from its natural background, its
id markings become strikingly obvious.
ny people have compared the colorful
metrical skin patterns to those on
ental carpets. Although unaggressive
unlikely to attack, this snake's bite
uld be dangerously venomous to anyone
ortunate enough to tread on one! In fact,
fangs of the gaboon viper are the
gest of any snake, up to 2 in (50 mm) in
ft (1.8 m) specimen.

· Gaboon viper

### HIDDEN DEPTHS

Luckily for this black caiman, it is often mistaken for
rocks as it lies in the muddy waters. Its ability to lie
unseen helps it when it is looking for food. It is
hunted for its skin and so is constantly threatened.

# Lots of legs

THE LEGS AND FEET of a reptile accurately reflect the animal's life-style. They are usually specifically adapted to the habitat in which the reptile lives. Desert lizards, for example, often have long scales fringing their toes, helping them to walk on soft sand. Climbing lizards tend to have very sharp claws, which allow them to grip even smooth surfaces firmly. Some climbing lizards, such as geckos, have gripping pads on the soles of their feet as well. Webbed feet and paddle-shaped limbs are found on some aquatic turtles. For other swimming reptiles, such as crocodiles and monitor lizards, the tail provides most of the propulsion, and the limbs are folded back out of the way.

**THE HARE AND THE TORTOISE**
In the famous Aesop fable, the hare is so confident of winn[ing] his race with the slow and ponderous tortoise, that he fa[lls] asleep by the wayside, and the tortoise crosses the finishing [line] first. It is certainly true that although tortoises are slow, th[ey] make steady progress and can travel very long distance[s], seldom stopping for a rest.

**LEGS OF ALL SORTS**
The powerful feet and legs of lizards such as monitors and plated lizards are good for digging. The sharp-clawed toes of the girdled lizards give the animals a strong grip when climbing, often on flaking rock surfaces. The slightly webbed back feet of the crocodilians help propel them through the water. The limbs of the smaller skinks are so small that they barely support the animal.

Caiman

Plated lizard

*All five toes spread out t[o] achieve maximum grip*

Monitor lizard

African girdled lizard

Blue-tongued skink

50

*Geckos have no trouble moving vertically or hanging horizontally*

**GET A GRIP**
The tokay, a fairly large gecko from eastern Asia, is so-called because one of the noises it makes sounds much like "tokay." This lizard is one of the best lizard climbers and has no difficulty scaling a wall, running across a ceiling, and even clinging to a sheet of glass. It grips by using pads on the underside of its fingers and toes. The pads are covered by microscopic, hairlike structures, which allow the gecko to cling to almost any surface. There may be as many as a million "hairs" on a tokay's pads, which rub the surface on which the animal is walking.

*Elongated body resembles that of a snake*

**LOSS OF LEGS**
This little glass lizard is often mistaken for a snake. It lives in rocky habitats or in thick vegetation. It has no front legs and only tiny, hardly visible remnants of back legs. These tiny back legs are called vestigial limbs, which are of little or no use to the animal. Many burrowing lizards have evolved in the same way. Without legs, these lizards can move around underground more easily.

*Vestigial limbs are of no use in movement, but the male may use them in courtship to stimulate the female*

**LITTLE LIMBS**
In most snakes, all traces of limbs have vanished. However, some of the more primitive groups, such as boas and pythons, have tiny remnants of the hip bones and hind limbs. The only external signs of these are small "claws" at the base of the tail, on either side of the vent, or anal opening.

Tokay gecko climbing

# Ground control

**M**OST LIZARDS RELY ON SWIFTNESS and agility to hunt and to escape trouble. They usually use all four limbs and can move at high speed. Their legs and feet are specially adapted to where they live. Turtles have no need for speed. Instead, they have powerful legs, which can carry the extra weight of a protective shell and propel them forward slowly but surely. In spite of having no legs, snakes also move very efficiently on land in a variety of ways. Their method of movement may change depending on their surroundings. Crocodilians are most at home in water, but when on land they crawl, dragging their bellies along the ground. Occasionally, smaller crocodiles can "gallop."

*Palm flexed against the ground*

*Back legs provide most of the thrust*

**LAND SPEED RECORD**
The six-lined racerunner, a type of lizard found in North America, holds the record for the highest speed reached by a reptile on land, 18 mph (29 kph). This record was set in 1941 in South Carolina.

Tegu lizard

### 3 TWO AT A TIME
When a lizard breaks into a trot, its body is supported by two legs at a time (the diagonal pairs). There may even be times when both front feet and one hind foot are off the ground.

**TWO LEGS ARE BETTER THAN FOUR**
This crested water dragon comes from Asia and lives mainly in trees growing near water. If disturbed when on the ground, it may rear up on its hind legs and run along upright for short bursts, its tail helping it to balance. This type of bipedal (two-legged) locomotion is also displayed by other lizards. These lizards can achieve greater speed running on two legs than they can on four.

*Long tail is used for balance*

Alerted crested water dragon standing on all four paws

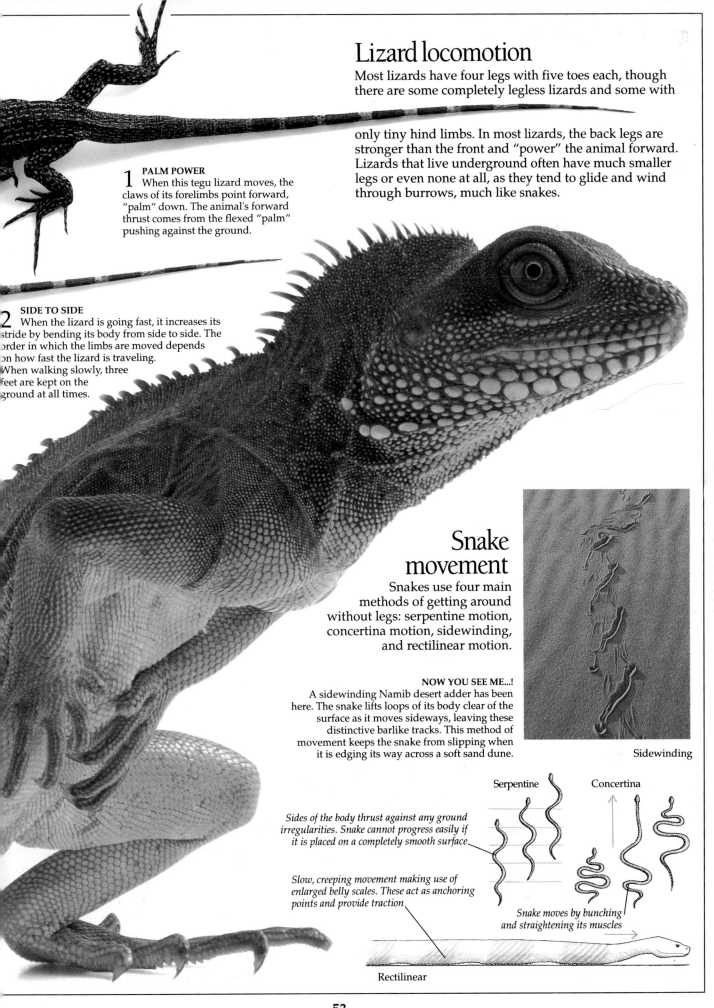

# Lizard locomotion

Most lizards have four legs with five toes each, though there are some completely legless lizards and some with only tiny hind limbs. In most lizards, the back legs are stronger than the front and "power" the animal forward. Lizards that live underground often have much smaller legs or even none at all, as they tend to glide and wind through burrows, much like snakes.

**1 PALM POWER**
When this tegu lizard moves, the claws of its forelimbs point forward, "palm" down. The animal's forward thrust comes from the flexed "palm" pushing against the ground.

**2 SIDE TO SIDE**
When the lizard is going fast, it increases its stride by bending its body from side to side. The order in which the limbs are moved depends on how fast the lizard is traveling. When walking slowly, three feet are kept on the ground at all times.

# Snake movement

Snakes use four main methods of getting around without legs: serpentine motion, concertina motion, sidewinding, and rectilinear motion.

**NOW YOU SEE ME...!**
A sidewinding Namib desert adder has been here. The snake lifts loops of its body clear of the surface as it moves sideways, leaving these distinctive barlike tracks. This method of movement keeps the snake from slipping when it is edging its way across a soft sand dune.

Sidewinding

Serpentine

Concertina

*Sides of the body thrust against any ground irregularities. Snake cannot progress easily if it is placed on a completely smooth surface*

*Slow, creeping movement making use of enlarged belly scales. These act as anchoring points and provide traction*

*Snake moves by bunching and straightening its muscles*

Rectilinear

## HIGHLY STRUNG

For much of the day, this mangrove snake lies high up in a tree. In the late afternoon or early evening, it slides into action, raiding nests for birds and their young. It is a rear-fanged snake, found in mangrove swamps and near rain forests.

# Life in the trees

MANY LIZARDS AND SNAKES are well adapted for life in trees and bushes. The toes of many arboreal or tree-dwelling lizards are often equipped with well developed claws for gripping tree trunks or special pads for clinging to smooth leaf surfaces. These lizards and some of the tree snakes often have long tails, which they twist around a branch, helping them to keep their balance. Some tree snakes have ridges on their belly scales, giving them additional gripping power. Arboreal reptiles are often found on isolated islands in the Pacific Ocean. It is believed they reached there on floating bits of vegetation.

## FURRY FAT FLIER

Like flying reptiles, the little flying squirrel glides rather than flies, using the folds of skin between its limbs. A lightweight animal, it sometimes eats so much it is unable to fly.

## HOT LIPS

This tree boa from South America has heat-sensitive pits in its lips so that it can find the roosting birds and bats on which it feeds. A stretchy body and strong tail make it particularly suited to this habitat. As it climbs, it reaches up and coils itself around a branch, hauling up the rest of its body as it goes.

*Coils act as anchor*

## FLYING ACE

This flying gecko has skin folds along its sides, legs, and tail; it also has webbed feet. Together these act as a parachute when the lizard glides through the air. Like the flying dragons, it uses its abilities to get out of trouble or to swoop down on food. The skin color and texture make the gecko difficult to detect when it sits on tree bark.

**HANGING ON**
An emerald green tree boa catches a bird. The snake uses a branch to support itself as it makes the kill.

**COOLING DOWN**
The trinket snake from India is a part-time tree-dweller. In hot weather it stays on the ground, sheltering in termite mounds or under rocks. However, in cooler weather it prefers to move up into trees and bushes. Although harmless to humans, it can look very frightening if threatened, swelling its neck and vibrating its tail as it strikes.

Garden lizard

**BLOODSUCKER**
The garden lizard's body is much like a chameleon's, and its tail is very long and slender. It can change color rapidly, especially its head, which sometimes turns red. In fact, the lips of some species become so red that these lizards have been nicknamed "bloodsuckers."

**DAREDEVIL DRAGONS**
Flying dragons have the same gifts in the air as the flying geckos, only their "wings" are flaps of skin stretched over elongated ribs. The wings fold back along the sides of the animal when not in use.

**DAY DUTY**
All geckos are good climbers, as the pads with clinging hairlike projections on their toes allow them to tackle almost any surface. This gecko is fairly unusual in that it is active by day; most geckos are active at night. Although day geckos eat a variety of insects and soft fruit, some seem to like the nectar that they find in palm flowers.

# Waterproofed

Aᴌᴛʜᴏᴜɢʜ ᴍᴏsᴛ ʀᴇᴘᴛɪʟᴇs ᴀʀᴇ land animals, several groups of reptiles live successfully in water. Crocodilians, a few lizards (such as the marine iguanas of the Galapagos Islands), some snakes (like the giant anaconda of South America), and terrapins and turtles all spend much of their lives submerged. Most reptiles have to return to dry land to lay their eggs, or the developing animal would drown. Some sea snakes, found mainly in the oceans around Asia, northern Australia, and the Pacific Islands, get around this problem by giving birth to live young that are immediately able to swim and come up for air. Different reptiles use their watery home in different ways: crocodilians swim, hunt, and cool off in it, and marine iguanas feed on algae growing on the submerged rocks.

**SNORKEL SNOUT**
When an alligator dives, special muscles and flaps close over the nostrils and ears. In calm water it needs to keep only its nose di above the surface. Another flap at the back of the throat stops th lungs from being flooded when the alligator opens its mouth under water. Its eyes are also waterproofed – in addition to w developed upper and lower lid: they are protected by a transpar shield that covers each eye.

*Eyes set high the he*

**TAIL WALKING**
If a crocodile is being chased, or if it is giving chase, it can move very fast, even leaping out of the water. This "tail walk," much like that of dolphins, demonstrates how graceful and at ease the animal is in water.

*Caiman lies still in water as a defense against predators and in order to catch prey*

Caiman

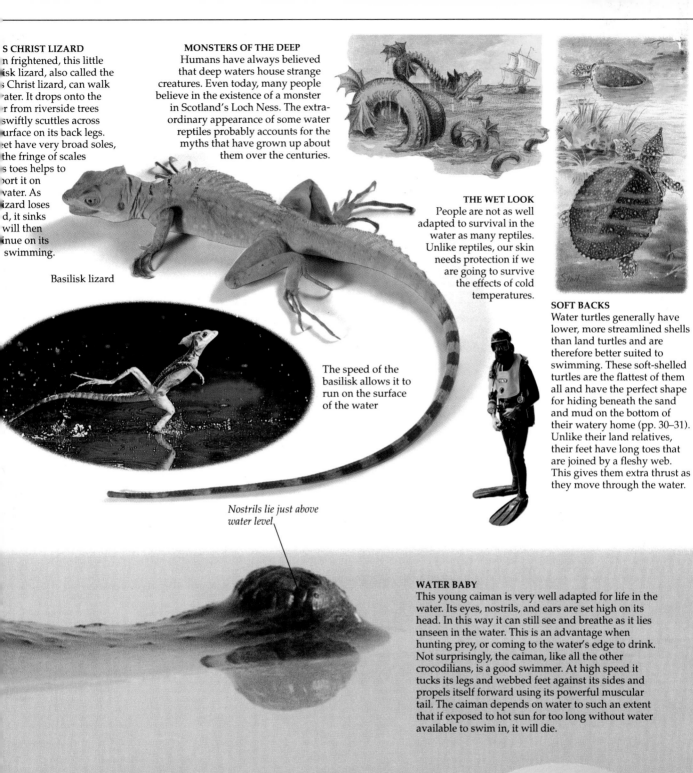

### ...S CHRIST LIZARD
...n frightened, this little
...isk lizard, also called the
...s Christ lizard, can walk
...ater. It drops onto the
...r from riverside trees
...swiftly scuttles across
...urface on its back legs.
...et have very broad soles,
...the fringe of scales
...s toes helps to
...ort it on
...ater. As
...izard loses
...d, it sinks
...will then
...nue on its
...swimming.

Basilisk lizard

### MONSTERS OF THE DEEP
Humans have always believed
that deep waters house strange
creatures. Even today, many people
believe in the existence of a monster
in Scotland's Loch Ness. The extra-
ordinary appearance of some water
reptiles probably accounts for the
myths that have grown up about
them over the centuries.

### THE WET LOOK
People are not as well
adapted to survival in the
water as many reptiles.
Unlike reptiles, our skin
needs protection if we
are going to survive
the effects of cold
temperatures.

### SOFT BACKS
Water turtles generally have
lower, more streamlined shells
than land turtles and are
therefore better suited to
swimming. These soft-shelled
turtles are the flattest of them
all and have the perfect shape
for hiding beneath the sand
and mud on the bottom of
their watery home (pp. 30–31).
Unlike their land relatives,
their feet have long toes that
are joined by a fleshy web.
This gives them extra thrust as
they move through the water.

The speed of the
basilisk allows it to
run on the surface
of the water

*Nostrils lie just above
water level*

### WATER BABY
This young caiman is very well adapted for life in the
water. Its eyes, nostrils, and ears are set high on its
head. In this way it can still see and breathe as it lies
unseen in the water. This is an advantage when
hunting prey, or coming to the water's edge to drink.
Not surprisingly, the caiman, like all the other
crocodilians, is a good swimmer. At high speed it
tucks its legs and webbed feet against its sides and
propels itself forward using its powerful muscular
tail. The caiman depends on water to such an extent
that if exposed to hot sun for too long without water
available to swim in, it will die.

### UNDERWATER BREATHING
All turtles have lungs, but aquatic
turtles can also breathe through their
skin and through the lining of the
throat. Some can tolerate very low
oxygen levels and can survive for
weeks under water, but this little red-
eared terrapin can last for no more than
two or three hours without surfacing.

Red-eared terrapin

# Best of enemies

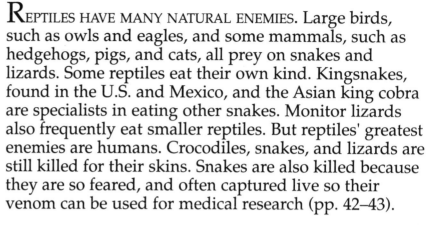

REPTILES HAVE MANY NATURAL ENEMIES. Large birds, such as owls and eagles, and some mammals, such as hedgehogs, pigs, and cats, all prey on snakes and lizards. Some reptiles eat their own kind. Kingsnakes, found in the U.S. and Mexico, and the Asian king cobra are specialists in eating other snakes. Monitor lizards also frequently eat smaller reptiles. But reptiles' greatest enemies are humans. Crocodiles, snakes, and lizards are still killed for their skins. Snakes are also killed because they are so feared, and often captured live so their venom can be used for medical research (pp. 42–43).

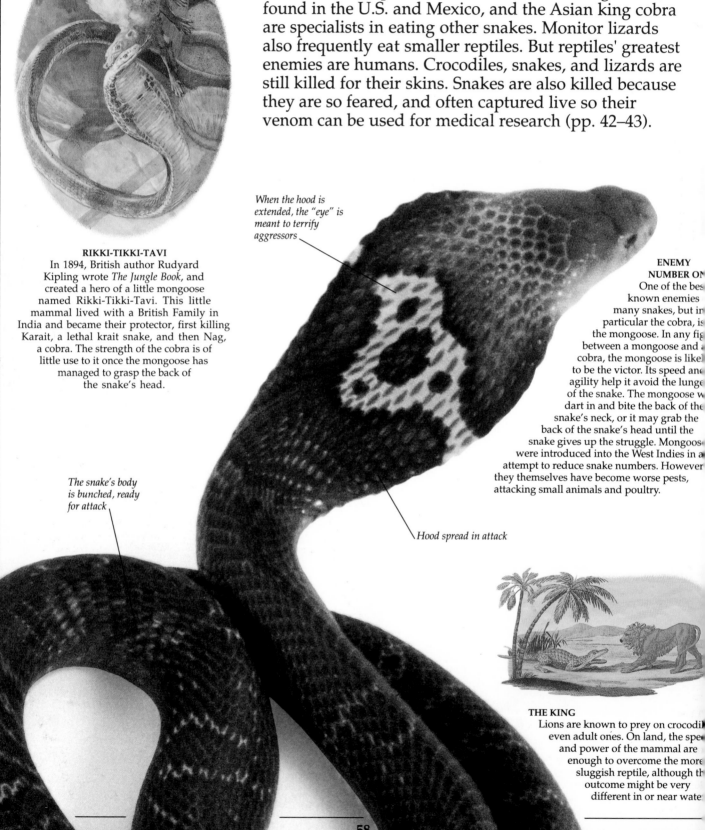

**RIKKI-TIKKI-TAVI**
In 1894, British author Rudyard Kipling wrote *The Jungle Book*, and created a hero of a little mongoose named Rikki-Tikki-Tavi. This little mammal lived with a British Family in India and became their protector, first killing Karait, a lethal krait snake, and then Nag, a cobra. The strength of the cobra is of little use to it once the mongoose has managed to grasp the back of the snake's head.

*When the hood is extended, the "eye" is meant to terrify aggressors*

*The snake's body is bunched, ready for attack*

*Hood spread in attack*

**ENEMY NUMBER ON**
One of the bes known enemies many snakes, but in particular the cobra, is the mongoose. In any fig between a mongoose and cobra, the mongoose is likel to be the victor. Its speed an agility help it avoid the lunge of the snake. The mongoose w dart in and bite the back of the snake's neck, or it may grab the back of the snake's head until the snake gives up the struggle. Mongoos were introduced into the West Indies in a attempt to reduce snake numbers. However they themselves have become worse pests, attacking small animals and poultry.

**THE KING**
Lions are known to prey on crocodil even adult ones. On land, the spe and power of the mammal are enough to overcome the more sluggish reptile, although th outcome might be very different in or near wate

Stiff hairs on the mongoose's back are raised to give added protection

Razor-sharp teeth attack the cobra at the back of the head

Body lightly poised on back paws for quick movement

**T FIRST**

secretary bird scares up possible prey, such as snakes, by stamping eet and flapping its wings. When a snake appears, attracted by the rations, the bird quickly kicks at it or stamps on it, at the same time ering the snake with its wings to keep it from moving into a position n which it can defend itself. In this way, it can even deal with dangerous kes such as adders and cobras. If stamping does not kill the snake, then bird will carry it high into the air and drop it onto hard ground.

**WAR DANCE**
In Indian mythology, the demon Kaliya changed himself into a cobra and killed many herdsmen in his search for the god Krishna. Finally, Krishna killed Kaliya and then danced on his head.

**TARZAN TRIUMPHS!**
Tarzan the apeman has no difficulty overpowering his reptilian enemy. In real life, a struggle between a crocodile and a human could have a very different ending. Although crocodiles are not usually man-eaters, they will certainly attack anyone foolish enough to stray near crocodile-infested rivers or breeding grounds.

# Just good friends

Cleaner fish

BECAUSE THE MAJORITY OF REPTILES are meat-eaters (pp. 38–39), the relationship between them and most other animals, even other reptiles, is usually that of predator and prey. However, some reptiles live side by side with other animals in a way that harms neither partner. Lizards and snakes, for example, together use termite mounds as incubators for their eggs. The gopher tortoise makes a burrow that is sometimes as much as 40 ft (12 m) long. This deep, cool burrow provides a permanent home or a temporary hiding place for many animals besides the tortoise. Other tortoise burrows have been found in which possums, raccoons, rabbits, lizards, and rats were living together happily. Even rattlesnakes are said to live peacefully with the other inhabitants in such a home.

## A HELPING HAND
The tuatara's existence on the remote islands off New Zealand is largely made possible by sea birds such as petrels and shearwaters (pp. 36–37). In fact, the tuatara sometimes shares its burrow with these birds. They cover the rocks and ground with their droppings, creating a perfect environment for large numbers of insects, including beetles and crickets, the tuatara's favorite food. However, it is an uneasy relationship, as tuataras eat nestling birds instead of insects if they get the chance.

Tuatara

Shearwater

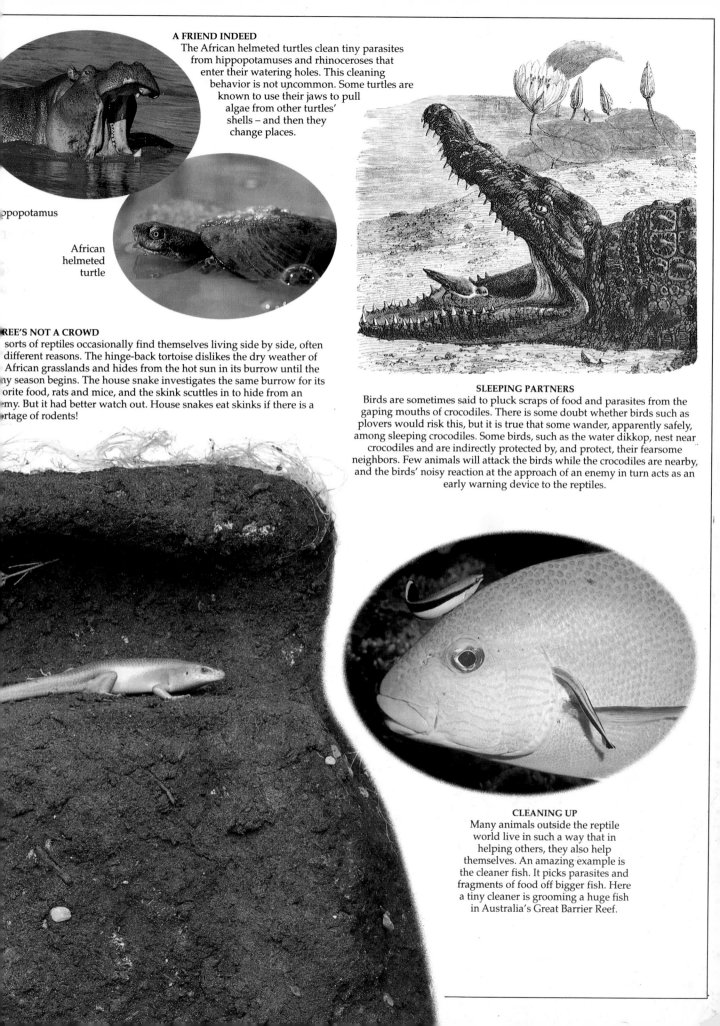

## A FRIEND INDEED
The African helmeted turtles clean tiny parasites from hippopotamuses and rhinoceroses that enter their watering holes. This cleaning behavior is not uncommon. Some turtles are known to use their jaws to pull algae from other turtles' shells – and then they change places.

Hippopotamus

African helmeted turtle

## ʀEE'S NOT A CROWD
sorts of reptiles occasionally find themselves living side by side, often different reasons. The hinge-back tortoise dislikes the dry weather of African grasslands and hides from the hot sun in its burrow until the ny season begins. The house snake investigates the same burrow for its orite food, rats and mice, and the skink scuttles in to hide from an my. But it had better watch out. House snakes eat skinks if there is a rtage of rodents!

## SLEEPING PARTNERS
Birds are sometimes said to pluck scraps of food and parasites from the gaping mouths of crocodiles. There is some doubt whether birds such as plovers would risk this, but it is true that some wander, apparently safely, among sleeping crocodiles. Some birds, such as the water dikkop, nest near crocodiles and are indirectly protected by, and protect, their fearsome neighbors. Few animals will attack the birds while the crocodiles are nearby, and the birds' noisy reaction at the approach of an enemy in turn acts as an early warning device to the reptiles.

## CLEANING UP
Many animals outside the reptile world live in such a way that in helping others, they also help themselves. An amazing example is the cleaner fish. It picks parasites and fragments of food off bigger fish. Here a tiny cleaner is grooming a huge fish in Australia's Great Barrier Reef.

# An eye to the future

UNLESS WE CHANGE THE WAY we live, many reptiles face extinction. Although it has taken over 150 million years for the once immensely varied reptiles to be reduced to just four groups, these now face a greater threat than ever before. The main cause for concern lies in the terrible destruction of their natural habitats. Many reptiles have specially adapted to life in some of the areas that are being lost at a frightening rate – for example the rain forests in the tropics and much of the shrubland of Europe. Although governments are now more aware of the situation and have agreed to help some severely threatened species, too little may have been done too late.

Snakeskin wallets

**SOUP, SOUP, BEAUTIFUL SOUP**
In some areas, reptiles are still very popular as a food for humans. Just a few years ago in the Caribbean 5,000 marine turtles were turned into 150,000 gallons (682,000 liters) of soup by just one food firm.

**SAFE – FOR HOW LONG?**
Although still fairly common, the giant skink of the Solomon Islands faces a problem shared by many other reptiles. Its habitat is being rapidly developed, and there is concern that as this happens many of these lizards will face extinction. This particular skink has further problems – it is commonly eaten in some areas. This very large animal spends nearly all its life in trees, as its monkey-like tail suggests. It eats mostly leaves and is active mainly at night.

**TOURIST TRAP**
This beautiful be in Turkey is one o last nesting sites o loggerhead turtles. Threatened by buildi development as a resu of the tourist trade, thes marine turtles face a very uncertain future, despite their long and varied history.

Baby big-headed turtle

**BIG HEAD**
The head of this turtle (well-named the big-headed turtle) is so large that it cannot be withdrawn into its shell. It is not yet acknowledged as being especially endangered, but because it looks so strange, it is often captured for the pet trade or used to make souvenirs. It lives in Southeast Asia, where during the day it spends its time buried in the gravel or under rocks in cool mountain streams.

An old engraving shows the head size in proportion to the body.

# Dirty dealing

In some parts of the world conservationists are trying to save reptiles, but many animals are still slaughtered to provide skins for the leather trade and souvenirs for tourists – including key rings made from the heads of hatchlings. Thousands of other reptiles have been collected by the pet trade, although in a few instances successful captive-breeding programs have helped to maintain the existence of rare species (pp. 36–37).

Siamese crocodile head keyring

Rattlesnake boot

**UNHAPPY PET**
The Pacific Island boa is found in a variety of habitats on the Solomon Islands, such as forests, farms, and near human dwellings. Although primarily a ground snake, it climbs well and is sometimes found in tree hollows, living on young lizards, rodents, and birds. This snake is sometimes kept as a pet, which is unfortunate, because in captivity it often "sulks" and refuses to eat. However, like the giant skink, it is threatened mainly by a disappearing habitat.

**DOWN THE LADDER**
Snakes are probably disappearing faster then any other group of vertebrates. They are at greater risk than ever in the 20th century, constantly in danger of being run over by cars. If something is not done to protect their habitats soon, we may be left with only board games and decorative models to remind us of these amazing animals.

Bead snake made by prisoners of war in 1916

# Index

# Acknowledgments

**Dorling Kindersley would like to thank:**
Trevor Smith and all the staff at Trevor Smith's Animal World for their help and enthusiasm.
Cyril Walker at the Natural History Museum for pages 8 and 9.
Keith Brown, Isolde McGeorge, and Chester Zoo for their kind permission to photograph tuataras.

**Picture credits**

t=top b=bottom l=left r=right
c=center

A.N.T./P & M Walton/N.H.P.A.: 10br; 56tl
Ancient Art & Architecture Collection: 34b
Aquila Photographics: 60ml
Ardea: /J.A. Bailey 22tr; /Jean-Paul Ferrero 48br
E.N. Arnold: 14bl
Biofotos/S. Summerhays: 23tr
Bridgeman Art Library: 26b; 62ml
British Museum (Natural History): 9m
Jane Burton: 25b
© Casterman: 40tr
Bruce Coleman Ltd: 33mr; /M. Fogden 7mr; /A. Stevens 7b, 42tr, 53br; /P. Davey 14mr, 38ml; /F. Lauting 19tr; /E. Bauer 19m; /D. Hughes 21b; /J. & D. Bartlett 28l; /C. Ott 33br; /J. Burton 38tl; /G. Zeisler 41ml; /B. Wood 42m; /J. Foote 42bc, 62tl; /R. Williams 46bm; /L. Lee Rue III 56tr; /M. Brulton 62-3t; /C. Frith 62t
Dorling Kindersley: 24m
Mary Evans Picture Library: 7tr; 8tl; 17tl;

18tl; 27tr; 38mr; 40mr; 43tl; 50-1; 57tm; 58tl
Sally & Richard Greenhill: 24mr
Robert Harding Picture Library: 14br; 16t; 47tl; 57mr
Michael Holford: 30tl; 34tr
Kobal Collection: 43tm
Frank Lane Picture Agency: 60m
Musee National d'Histoire Naturelle, Paris: 30ml
National Museum of Wales: 30mr
N.H.P.A.: 57ml; 61tm
Natural Science Photos: /P.H. & S.L. Ward 32
Oxford Scientific Films: 52tl; 61tl; /S. Osolinski 18m; /K. Atkinson 37br; /Z. Leszczynski 41mr, 46bl; /J. Gerlach 42bl; /Stouffer Productions 54m; /S. Mills 62br
Planet Earth Pictures: 60tl; 61br; /K. Lucas 20m; /P. Scoones 37tr
Ann Ronan Picture Library: 22bm
South Kensington Antiques: 62bc
Frank Spooner Pictures: 28br
Syndication International: 6ml
By Courtesy of the Board of Trustees of the Victoria & Albert Museum: 34m
Wildlight Photo Agency/Oliver Strewe: 21tr
Jerry Young: 42c, 43c

**Illustrations by Andrew Macdonal[d]**
13; 17; 21; 38; 41; 42; 47; 51; 53